T5-AFW-435

SUSTAINABLE DESIGN II

Sustainable Design II
©2007
by the National Council of Architectural Registration Boards.
All rights reserved. No part of this document may be reproduced, stored in a retrieval
system or transmitted for reproduction without the prior permission of the publisher.

National Council of Architectural Registration Boards (NCARB)
1801 K Street
Washington, DC 20006
202/783-6500
www.ncarb.org

ISBN 978-0-941575-53-9
Printed in the United States of America

This monograph was published in December 2007.

FOREWORD

This is NCARB's twenty-second monograph on a topic of special interest to professionals in architecture and related fields. While this initiative is specifically designed to help architects meet the continuing and professional development requirements of state boards for continued professional licensure, it is also suitable for other professionals as well–either to meet the continuing education requirements of their particular profession or to broaden their general knowledge of the subject. Monographs published by NCARB are also accepted by the American Institute of Architects (AIA) to meet its continuing education requirement for maintenance of membership in the institute.

Sustainable Design II is another in the continuing series of monographs produced by NCARB's Professional Development Program (PDP). In 2001 NCARB published *Sustainable Design* to provide an overview of the concept and principles of sustainability to architects. Since that publication date, sustainable design has entered into the mainstream as a significant environmental and economic force in building design, construction and development. Our latest volume focuses more on the specific tools and techniques that architects need to master the design of more environmentally responsible buildings. This book includes a review of metrics, rating systems such as USBC's LEED Green Building Rating System, cost analyses, and integrated design strategies. Additional detailed readings on the subject of sustainable design, including *Indoor Environment* and *Energy Conscious Architecture* can also be obtained through NCARB's monograph series at www.ncarb.org.

NCARB's Committee on Professional Development selects the topic, reviews content, and prepares quiz questions for each new monograph. The subject matter covered in each monograph is intended to present new information, deemed important to the public's health, safety and welfare, for use by the architect in his or her practice. NCARB will continue to release new monographs on a myriad of topics of concern to architects. The committee also reviews titles of previously published monographs for timeliness and applicability of general concepts. When appropriate, monographs are revised and republished.

NCARB welcomes your comments and questions about *Sustainable Design II* and the Professional Development Program in general. Please let us know what other topics you would like to see addressed. Thank you for your participation.

ABOUT THE AUTHORS

Muscoe Martin, AIA, LEED, is an architect and founding principal of M²
Architecture, a design, research, and consulting firm focused on integrating ecology,
aesthetics, and health in the built environment. Prior to forming M²A in 2005, he
was a senior associate at Wallace Roberts & Todd and, from 1996–2002, was a principal with Susan Maxman & Partners. A LEED Accredited Professional since 2001,
he has been involved in many green and LEED projects.

Martin has a Masters of Architecture from the University of Pennsylvania, and a
Bachelor of Arts from Princeton University. He is on the faculty of the University of
Pennsylvania School of Design, where he teaches ecological design, and has lectured
extensively throughout the United States. He is a member of the Board of Directors
of the United States Green Building Council (USGBC), past chairman of the AIA's
Committee on the Environment, and serves on the USGBC LEED Faculty and the
LEED Steering Committee.

Gregory Franta, FAIA, is the principal architect for Rocky Mountain Institute (RMI)
and leader of RMI's Built Environment Team. He has provided services on more
than 800 energy-efficient and environmentally sound projects, including offices, laboratories, educational buildings, health facilities, libraries, homes (including the
White House), and other buildings—many considered the most energy efficient in
the United States. His work also includes planning for sustainable cities, neighborhoods, and campuses. Franta is the recipient of the 1998 AIA Colorado Architect of
the Year Award and has served on the National Board of Directors for the American
Institute of Architects, is a cofounder (past chairman) of the AIA Committee on the
Environment, and represents AIA in the Union of International Architects Working
Group on "Energy and Architecture." He is also a LEED Accredited Professional, a
LEED trainer for the USGBC, part of the LEED certification team for the USGBC,
and a recipient of a 2006 USGBC Leadership award. RMI is an independent, entre-
preneurial, nonprofit organization that fosters the efficient and restorative use of
resources to make the world secure, just, prosperous, and life-sustaining. RMI staff
show businesses, communities, individuals, and governments how to create more
wealth and employment, protect and enhance natural and human capital, increase
profit and competitive advantage, and enjoy many other benefits—largely by doing
what they do far more efficiently. RMI's work is independent, nonadversarial, and
trans-ideological, with a strong emphasis on market-based solutions. RMI's three
research and consulting teams, the Built Environment Team, the Energy and
Resources Team, and the Breakthrough Design Team, provide a broad range of consulting services to businesses and organizations of all sizes.

ACKNOWLEDGEMENTS

The authors would like to thank all the colleagues who provided case studies and
images for this monograph including Scott Kelly of Re:Vision Architecture; Tavis
Dockwiller of Veridian Landscape Studios; Jose Alminana of Andropogon Associates;
Tom Cahill of Cahill and Associates; Michelle Robinson of Wallace Roberts & Todd;
and Don Horn from the U.S. General Services Administration. Thanks are also
owed to research assistants Jennifer vander Veer, Milena Bica, and Caroline Fluhrer
and to Taryn Holowka and the communications staff of the USGBC.

INTRODUCTION

Much has happened in the field of green building design since the 2001 publication of NCARB's previous Professional Development Program publication, *Sustainable Design*. Many more buildings have been built incorporating sustainable design principles, and some of these have been operating for long enough to have their performance measured and assessed. Increasing concern about global climate change and other ecological problems tied to building construction and land use has led to an expanded interest in sustainable design beyond a committed minority to a broad section of mainstream owners, architects, developers, and builders. Articles on green buildings appear daily in the popular and trade press. There are few professionals who do not have at least a basic understanding of the effects on environmental and human health of building construction—site disturbance, energy and water consumption, waste production, materials manufacture, and interior air quality.

The 2001 monograph described the theory of sustainable design, including the overall benefits to the planet, society, and individuals, and provided an overview of the process of designing sustainable buildings. This new monograph focuses more on the "nuts and bolts" of green building design—the specific tools and techniques that architects need to master in order to design more environmentally responsible buildings. These tools include metrics, rating systems, cost analyses, and integrated design strategies.

The first section—"What Have We Learned?"—summarizes some of the important developments in the field of sustainable design since the previous monograph was written, such as the growth of the U.S. Green Building Council (USGBC) and its Leadership in Energy and Environmental Design (LEED) rating system and the AIA's ambitious commitment in 2005 to reducing building energy use and greenhouse gas emissions substantially. This section also includes a review of the most informative recent research on the benefits of green buildings.

Thanks to LEED and other rating systems, there is a growing awareness of performance metrics used to assess a project's environmental and health impact, although these metrics are not yet in common use by the profession. The section "Performance Metrics for Sustainable Design" reviews a number of these measures related to energy, water, land use, materials, waste, and indoor environmental quality. Wider use and understanding of these metrics is necessary to move sustainable design from vague qualitative design approaches to more objective performance benchmarks. This adoption of solid, quantitative criteria will be the next stage in the evolution of sustainable design.

Perhaps the most important development since 2001 has been the growth of the USGBC's LEED Green Building Rating System. LEED has become a significant influence in the real estate, design, and construction industries and is being used by a wide variety of clients including governments, institutions, developers, and private corporations. It is rapidly becoming the de facto definition of green building design. The section "Building Rating Systems" focuses heavily on LEED and its growing number of "products" and application guides, and also reviews other rating systems available both in the United States and elsewhere.

The cost of sustainable design is a common challenge for architects and their clients. The section "Economics of Sustainable Buildings" reviews the cost question and describes the life cycle costing methods that are at the core of sustainable design. A summary of three major studies on costs and benefits of green buildings provides the results and conclusions of the most widely published information from the industry.

The last section, "Integrated Design," is the most important in many ways because it is based on the accumulated knowledge of many experienced green-building practitioners. It was written by researchers and architects at the Rocky Mountain Institute (RMI), an organization with a long experience on the cutting edge of sustainable design and development. This section describes the process of designing using a collaborative, systems-based approach and explains the common barriers to this way of designing. The benefits of integrated design are illustrated by a detailed case study that demonstrates how the process was used to deliver a high-performance green design for a large government office building.

A brief word on terminology: many people differentiate between the terms "sustainable design" and "green building design." The word "sustainability" means different things in different contexts and in other industries. For the purposes of this publication, these terms are used more or less interchangeably to refer to building and community designs that are environmentally responsible and promote health and productivity for their users and occupants.

James Hartzfeld, former chairman of the USGBC, has called green building "the most successful environmental movement of our time." Whether you believe this claim or not, there are many indicators suggesting that sustainable design has entered the mainstream as a significant environmental and economic force in building design, construction, and development. Architects have been at the forefront of this movement since its beginnings. This monograph provides the tools for the next generation of sustainable architects to continue this leadership and to design buildings that are cost effective and measurably green.

WHAT HAVE WE LEARNED?

The most important recent developments in the field of sustainable design fall in three general categories.

Current Trends In Practice. Indications of the tremendous growth in interest in environmentally friendly buildings can be found throughout the industry in statements by mainstream organizations like the American Institute of Architects (AIA), in government mandates and incentives, and in the dramatic growth of the USGBC and its LEED Green Building Rating System.

Research and Performance Data. The growing interest in sustainable design has catalyzed several research activities. The results, while still limited in scope and number, demonstrate that sustainable design can provide measurable and cost effective benefits to building owners, occupants, and the planet.

Design Process. The evidence from the field suggests that conventional design processes need to change to deliver cost-effective green buildings that perform as intended. A "whole-building integrated-design" process that emphasizes greater collaboration among the design disciplines, particularly in the early phases of design, has been shown to be more effective at producing buildings that meet their environmental, programmatic, and budgetary goals.

CURRENT PRACTICE TRENDS
Architecture Profession's Commitment

In 2005, the AIA Board of Directors adopted a resolution committing the Institute to:

"Promote sustainable design including resource conservation to achieve a minimum 50 percent reduction from the current level of consumption of fossil fuels used to construct and operate new and renovated buildings by the year 2010, and promote further reductions of remaining fossil fuel consumption by 10 percent or more in each of the following five years" (AIA 2005).

These ambitious goals by the AIA reflect the architecture profession's growing understanding of the effects of building construction and operation on the environment in general and, in particular, the impacts related to global climate change. This statement also reflects the AIA's recognition of the potential for sustainable design to reduce or eliminate these negative environmental effects, and an acceptance of the responsibility to "alter our profession's actions" (AIA 2005).

The AIA's Committee on the Environment (COTE) was one of the first groups to advocate for environmentally sustainable design, even before USGBC was founded. COTE has recognized green building designs that successfully combine technical and environmental performance with

FIGURE 1A
AIA Committee on the Environment Top 10 award winner: Cusano Environmental Education Center by Susan Maxman & Partners. *Photo courtesy Barry Halkin.*

AMERICAN INSTITUTE OF ARCHITECTS
HIGH PERFORMANCE BUILDING POSITION STATEMENTS
Sustainable Architectural Practice

The AIA recognizes a growing body of evidence that demonstrates current planning, design, construction, and real estate practices contribute to patterns of resource consumption that seriously jeopardize the future of the earth's population. Architects need to accept responsibility for their role in creating the built environment and, consequently, believe we must alter our profession's actions and encourage our clients and the entire design and construction industry to join with us to change the course of the planet's future.

Explanation

Altering current practices of design and construction to realize significant reductions in the use of natural resources, nonrenewable energy sources, and waste production and promote regeneration of natural resources will require a multiple-year effort in conjunction with clients, industry partners, and concerned organizations.

To achieve these changes, the AIA will act through all its Board Committees, Knowledge Communities, Task Forces, Working Groups, and related activities to:

1. Promote sustainable design including resource conservation to achieve a minimum 50 percent reduction from the current level of consumption of fossil fuels used to construct and operate new and renovated buildings by the year 2010, and promote further reductions of remaining fossil fuel consumption by 10 percent or more in each of the following five years;
2. Collaborate with other national and international organizations, the scientific research community, public health community, and industry leaders engaged in issues related to sustainable/ restorative design to facilitate the dialogue, share knowledge, and accelerate the rate of change for all those seeking to improve the industry's current practices and utilize integrated approaches to achieve a sustainable future;
3. Develop and promote the integration of sustainability into the curricula for education of architects and architectural students to enhance their design skills;
4. Develop standards for the architectural profession that incorporate greater sustainability into design, education, management, and licensure standards and provide resources to assist integrating these standards into the daily practices of all architects;
5. Promote documentation of the measurable contributions resulting from implemented sustainable design and construction approaches to the health of humankind and the planet to promote the value and achievements of increased use of sustainable design;
6. Promote research by industry, scientific, and governmental entities to provide the design and construction industry with full life-cycle assessment data for all products and assemblies used in the construction of the built environment at every scale in order to facilitate decision-making and communicate benefits to all;
7. Promote the AIA's building performance design targets to local, state, and national governments;
8. Communicate possible beneficial economics of environmentally responsible design to both public and private sector clients; and
9. Assume a global role as advocates for sustainable design, freely sharing knowledge and actively promoting sustainable practice throughout the world.

FIGURE 1B

AIA Committee on the Environment Top 10 award winner: ABN-AMRO Bank World Headquarters by Pei Cobb Freed & Partners. *Photo courtesy Luc Boegly/Pei Cobb Freed & Partners.*

aesthetics through its annual Top Ten Awards (http://aiatopten.org/hpb/). This awards program, begun in the late 1990s, has become one of the most coveted sources of recognition in the green building field. The size and reputation of the firms represented in the list of winning entries indicates that the architecture profession is embracing green design as more than a fad.

Business Trends

In a 2006 publication on the marketing and business opportunities for sustainable design and construction, McGraw Hill reported that green building represented "approximately a $3.3 billion industry." They projected that by 2010, the green building market would grow to "between $10.2 billion and $20.5 billion," representing 5 to 10 percent of all noncommercial construction in the United States (McGraw Hill Construction Research and Analytics 2006). These numbers are based on surveys of architecture/ engineering/ construction firms as well as owners and real estate developers.

The report presents a number of insights into the motivations and reasons owners are asking for sustainable design. The top two reasons for deciding to pursue green building are "lowering lifecycle costs" and "being part of an industry that values the environment." Interestingly, the responses were split nearly equally between these two motivating factors. This was true for all respondents (owners, architects, engineers, and contractors), suggesting one reason for the growing acceptance of sustainable design: it appeals to two sides of human nature.

FIGURE 2

Projected market values are based on McGraw-Hill Construction's nonresidential construction starts data for 2005 and forecasted starts through 2006. *Source: McGraw-Hill Construction, Green Building SmartMarket Report, 2006.*

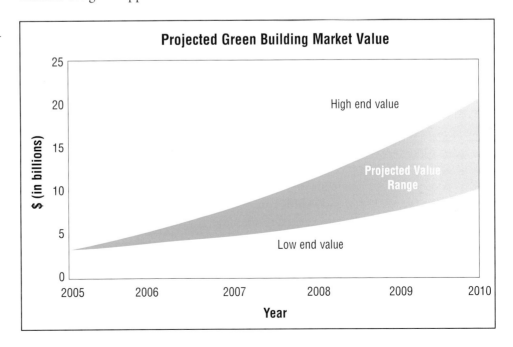

Other data from the McGraw Hill publication suggest that it is not the design community pushing green design on their clients. In fact, it appears to be the other way around, with "client demand" being the largest "trigger" for architects and engineers to adopt green building practices. Owners are generally focused on the bottom line; their three most important business reasons for building green are "lower operating costs, higher building value, and better 10-year costs."

The conclusions of the McGraw Hill report are supported by the growing number of news articles on green buildings appearing daily around the country, including feature pieces on the benefits of sustainable design in mainstream business publications such as the *Wall Street Journal, Forbes,* and *Fortune.* The business community has begun to accept sustainable architecture as a legitimate approach to design and construction that has multiple benefits to the financial bottom line as well as to the planet.

USGBC and LEED

The impressive growth of the USGBC over the past few years and its expanding influence on the industry are strong indicators of the broad acceptance of sustainable design. Membership in the USGBC increased from a few hundred in the mid-1990s to more than 7,300 member companies in 2006. This increase has been mainly fueled by the design professions, with architecture firms leading this group, along with product manufacturers and real estate developers.

With the rise in membership has come a substantially increased staff, budget, and stature in the industry. The increased visibility has also brought greater scrutiny by a variety of groups from government agencies, legislatures, and industry associations. Most of these groups have been supportive of the goals and tactics of USGBC, but some have been antagonistic. The latter have been mainly led by industry groups who perceive USGBC and its principal tool, LEED, to be unfair or detrimental to their business interests. On the other hand, there are advocacy organizations who counter that LEED does not go far enough to protect the environment.

The number of projects that are using the LEED Green Building Rating System has increased dramatically. Over 60 million square feet [5.6 million square meters] of buildings have been officially certified by USGBC with another 450 million square feet [42 million square meters] registered and moving through the LEED process (http://www.usgbc.org). This does not include projects that are using LEED unofficially as a guideline and checklist for incorporating green design strategies. Further evidence that sustainable design has penetrated beyond the expected "early adopters" such as environmental groups and government agencies is in the growing use of LEED in large projects for corporations and real estate developers. The USGBC reports that over 25 percent of the clients of LEED-registered projects are for-profit corporations.

More than 24,000 individuals have passed the USGBC LEED Accredited Professional Exam. These include architects, engineers, interior designers, contractors,

---

ABOUT USGBC

The U.S. Green Building Council (USGBC) is a nonprofit organization founded in 1993 to promote buildings that are environmentally responsible, profitable, and healthy places to live and work. Its more than 6,300 member firms and organizations come from every sector of the building industry including architects, engineers, contractors, developers, product manufacturers, service providers, clients, and governments. Their flagship initiative is the Leadership in Energy and Environmental Design (LEED) Green Building Rating System. LEED is a voluntary, consensus-based national standard for developing high-performance, sustainable buildings. USGBC also organizes the annual Greenbuild International Conference and Expo. The USGBC's core purpose is to transform the way buildings and communities are designed, built, and operated, enabling an environmentally and socially responsible, healthy, and prosperous environment that improves the quality of life in our communities. (http://www.usgbc.org)

FIGURE 3A

U.S. Green Building Council membership growth. *Source: USGBC.*

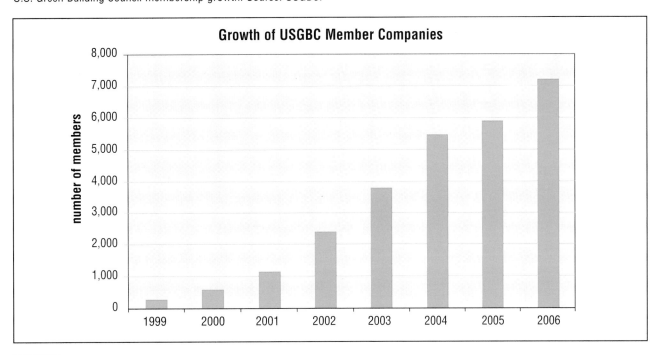

FIGURE 3B

Distribution by profession of USGBC members. *Source: USGBC.*

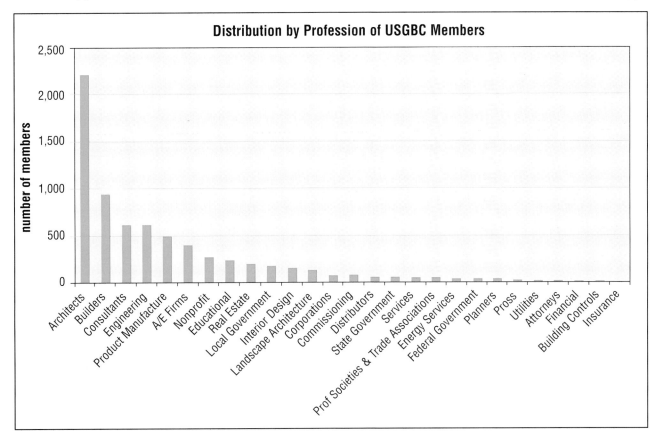

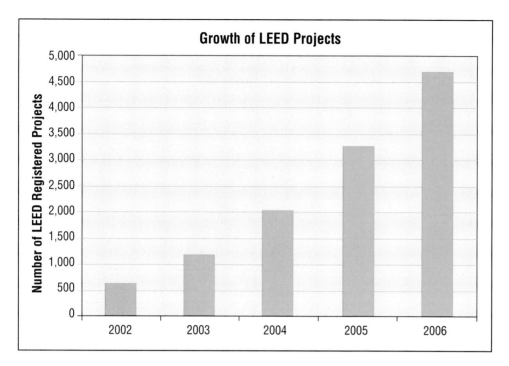

Growth of LEED Projects

FIGURE 4

Growth of LEED projects since 2000. *Source: USGBC.*

product representatives, teachers, and other professionals involved in the design and construction industry. This rapidly increasing number is perhaps the strongest indicator that the industry recognizes the value of credentials related to green building design. Many firms display the number of LEED-accredited professionals prominently in their web sites and marketing materials.

Government Mandates and Incentives

Governments, at all levels, have recognized the benefits of sustainable design to the environment as well as to their own balance sheet. Over the past several years, federal, state, and municipal governments have been among the most aggressive promoters of green building design. Many have adopted green building standards for their own capital projects. In addition, a wide variety of incentives has been developed for privately funded buildings, such as tax credits, rebates, and other considerations.

Many federal agencies, such as the General Services Administration, the Department of Defense, the Environmental Protection Agency, the Forest Service, and the National Park Service, have revised their design and construction standards to include green design. This includes, at a minimum, "environmentally preferable purchasing" and energy-efficient design. Many now require LEED certification, as well.

Around the country, several states have adopted green design standards for government-funded construction. These are concentrated in the West and include Arizona, California, Washington, and Nevada. Eastern states have also begun to adopt green guidelines, including Maine and Maryland. A growing number of cities are also requiring LEED for use in their own municipal buildings, including San Francisco, New York City, Seattle, Portland, OR, and Austin, TX.

The adoption of green building principles by government has been a significant factor in the industry because of the large amount and scope of government capital

FIGURE 5A

Growth of the number LEED Accredited Professionals since 2001, when the LEED exams were first given. *Source: USGBC.*

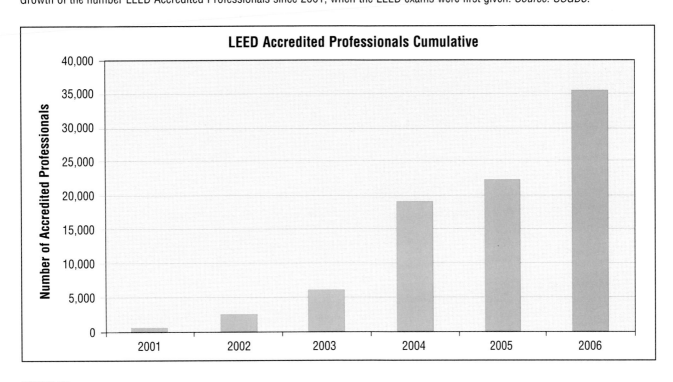

FIGURE 5B

Distribution by profession of LEED Accredited Professionals. *Source: USGBC.*

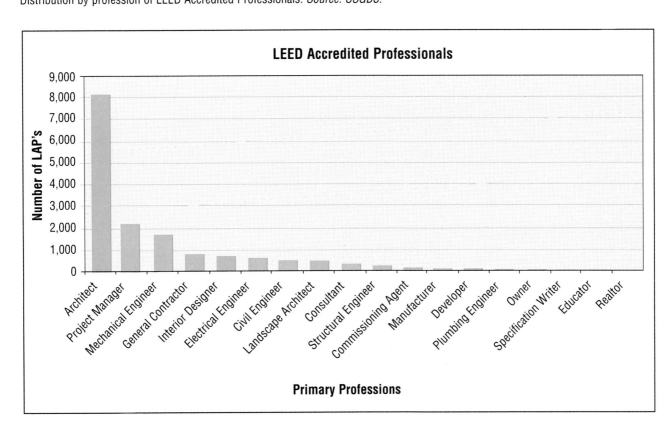

spending. This market is served by many of the country's biggest design and construction firms. By introducing green building requirements in their requests for proposals (RFPs), governments have encouraged these large, mainstream companies to educate themselves and their staff about sustainable design, and to develop the capacity and infrastructure to deliver green buildings.

FIGURE 6
The San Francisco Federal Building, designed by Morphosis, in association with SmithGroup, is expected to receive a Silver LEED rating. *Rendering courtesy of Morphosis.*

This has rippled down through the industry into the subcontractor and subconsultant sectors, as well as to smaller builders and architecture firms.

While the number of government-funded capital projects is very large, the private-sector market, with the associated environmental influence, is still larger. To encourage the design and construction of green buildings by private homeowners, corporations, and developers, many governments have instituted incentive programs. Many of these incentives are tax credits and/or rebates to the builder and/or owner for incorporating sustainable strategies or technologies in their buildings. Other jurisdictions have developed more creative encouragement for sustainable design including incentives that permit the construction of larger buildings than would otherwise be allowed by the zoning code, or even faster permit review. These incentive programs are expanding around the country and are no doubt contributing to the increase in green building. The Interstate Renewable Energy Council (http://www.dsireusa.org/) maintains a web site that lists many of these programs. The USGBC web site also has a listing of LEED Initiatives in Governments and Schools.

RESEARCH AND PERFORMANCE DATA

Because the first generation of green buildings built in the late 1990s has now been operating for several years, actual operating data and post-occupancy performance assessments are available. Public and institutional buildings and even some private projects have been studied and the case study results published. This information, while limited, provides critically useful feedback on what is working and what is not. In addition to these case studies, other research on the costs and benefits of green buildings has been produced and can provide guidance and direction for design teams and clients looking for cost-effective strategies to incorporate green design into their projects.

The growth in construction of green buildings over the past 10 years has provided plenty of case-study data. While there is not yet a formal, dedicated program to collect performance data on LEED-certified and other green buildings, there are several sources of case-study data. The

---

STATE AND LOCAL GOVERNMENTS THAT PROVIDE INCENTIVES FOR LEED BUILDINGS:

TAX INCENTIVES

Maryland

Nevada

New York

Oregon

Baltimore County, MD

Chatham County, GA

Cincinnati, OH

Pasadena, CA

DENSITY BONUS

Acton, MA

Arlington, VA

EXPEDITED PERMIT REVIEW

Chicago, IL

Gainesville, FL

Issaquah, WA

Santa Monica, CA

Sarasota County, FL

GRANTS

Cincinnati, OH

Pennsylvania Public Schools

Santa Monica, CA

FIGURE 7

The 350,000-square-foot [32,500-m^2] Jack Evans Police Headquarters serves as administration offices for the Dallas Police Department. Designed by PSA-Dewberry Inc., the project received a Silver LEED certification. *Photo courtesy Mark Trew Photography.*

NEW YORK'S GREEN BUILDING TAX CREDIT

In May 2000, New York became the first state to offer tax credits to developers who build green buildings. This innovative tax law is intended to encourage the real estate and construction industries to adopt green practices on a large scale by providing tax credits to building owners and tenants who invest in increased energy efficiency, recycled and recyclable materials, and improved indoor air quality.

The credit allows builders who meet energy goals and use environmentally preferable materials to claim up to $3.75 per square foot [$40.36/m^2] for interior work and $7.50 per square foot [$80.73/m^2] for exterior work against their state tax bill. To qualify for the credit, a building must be certified by a licensed architect or engineer, and must meet specific requirements for energy use, materials selection, indoor air quality, waste disposal, and water use. In new buildings, this means energy use cannot exceed 65 percent of use permitted under the New York State energy code; in rehabilitated buildings, energy use cannot exceed 75 percent. Ventilation and thermal comfort must meet certain requirements, and building materials, finishes, and furnishings must contain high percentages of recycled content and renewable source material and cannot exceed specified maximum levels of toxicity. Waste disposal and water use must also comply with criteria set forth in the new law.

Ten percent of the cost of ozone-friendly air-conditioning equipment, 30 percent of the installed cost of fuel cells, and 100 percent of the cost of built-in photovoltaic (PV) solar panels may also be recouped through the credit. Fuel cells, which emit only carbon dioxide and water, and PV panels, which convert sunlight directly to electricity with no emissions at all, both carry high up-front costs compared to conventional energy delivery technologies.

USGBC web site maintains a list of all LEED-registered and -certified projects. LEED-registered projects have only begun the process of certification and may be anywhere in the process from design through construction. Construction must be complete for buildings to achieve the final certification. Those applying for certification are required to submit case study information; however because LEED is a design certification, there is no actual performance data collected (except for projects certified under the LEED for Existing Buildings (LEED-EB) Rating System, described later). The U.S. Department of Energy (DOE) maintains a "High Performance Buildings Database" (http://www.eere.energy.gov/buildings/database/), which features over 150 detailed case studies. While a number of these do include actual measured performance data, most report only the design projections for energy use and other performance metrics. This is one area where the industry needs to do a better job–collecting and publishing real-world data.

In addition to developing the High Performance Buildings Database, DOE has conducted detailed post occupancy monitoring of six early, ground-breaking green buildings (Torcellini 2006). These projects were all designed in the 1990s and completed around the year 2000. They represent a variety of building types including office buildings, a classroom building, a retail center, and a visitor center. While these studies focus almost exclusively on energy consumption, they are very useful in identifying design, construction, and operational strategies that have worked and those that haven't.

The results of the monitoring study are very promising. Each building uses much less energy than a comparable code-compliant building. The energy consumption ranged from 25 to 70 percent lower than code. However, all six buildings used more energy than predicted during design. Several reasons were proposed for this discrepancy including inaccurate assumptions about actual building use and occupant behavior, lower savings from day-

FIGURE 8

The Zion National Park Visitor Center is one of six green buildings whose performance has been monitored in detail by the U.S. Department of Energy. *Photo courtesy of the National Park Service.*

lighting strategies and larger than expected "plug loads" (non-HVAC equipment using electricity).

The sidebar summarizes the lessons learned from this DOE research. One of the most surprising conclusions is that "off-the-shelf" technologies are available today to achieve low-energy buildings. In other words, we don't need to experiment with new or untried systems to design energy-efficient structures. Great improvements have been made in many building technologies over the past decade, including glass, lighting and lighting controls, and HVAC equipment. Unfortunately many of these available products are not being used. For instance, improved window systems, such as low-e glazing, are mature technologies and provide energy savings in most parts of the country, yet are found in less than 40 percent of new home construction and an astonishingly low 17 percent of new commercial buildings in the United States (U.S. Climate Change Technology Program 2005).

Clearly, expanded education about these products is needed to drive greater market penetration of these state-of-the-shelf (the best of what is widely available) technologies. Knowing when and how to use substitute technologies, like advanced windows, is a key part of green design. However, achieving the very ambitious energy-efficient goals needed to address climate change requires the proper application *and* combination of these systems and products for a given climate, location, building type, and client. The DOE report encourages a design process that determines the optimal assembly of building systems, shell, and massing. This is the one of the goals of "integrated whole-building design," whose importance to achieving energy efficiency is another of the DOE lessons learned, along with the benefits of setting measurable goals at the beginning of the project. Both of these points are taken up in detail later.

The Pacific Northwest region has been a major market for LEED-certified buildings. The Cascadia regional chapter of the USGBC has taken advantage of this concentration of green projects in their area to gather post-occupancy data on a small number of LEED-certified buildings. The eleven projects surveyed by Cascadia had all been occupied for at least one year, providing data through a full seasonal cycle. The study reveals similar findings to the DOE research but also includes performance on water consumption and the results of an occupant sur-

LESSONS LEARNED FROM DOE CASE STUDIES

Owners provide the main motivation for low-energy buildings. The owner was the driving force in each case. Each owner set the goals and made decisions to keep the project on track. The architects and engineers strived to meet the goals of the building owners, which resulted in the need for the whole-building design process.

Setting measurable energy saving goals at the outset of the project is crucial to realizing low-energy buildings. In the case studies, all the owners and design teams set aggressive energy saving goals at the outset. The goals ranged from 40 percent better than code to net-zero energy performance. In general, the teams that set the strongest energy performance goals and used energy simulation to understand the energy impacts of design decisions had the best energy performance.

Many decisions are not motivated by cost. Building owners make decisions based on values. Quite often owners will pay for features they really want in a building—this is especially true of architectural features. Conversely, if an owner does not want a feature, cost is often used as the reason to eliminate it.

Today's technologies can substantially change how buildings perform. Properly applied off-the-shelf or "state-of-the-shelf" (the best of what is widely available) technologies are available to achieve low-energy buildings. However, these strategies must be applied together and properly integrated in the design, installation, and operation to realize energy savings. There is no single efficiency measure or checklist of measures to achieve low-energy buildings.

A whole-building design approach is a good way to lower energy use and cost. An integrated whole-building approach begins with a design team that is committed to the energy goals. The building must be engineered as a system if the technologies are to be integrated in design and operation. This includes using computer simulations to help guide the design process; these simulations can perform trade-off analysis to examine energy impacts of architecture choices and heating, ventilation, air-conditioning, and lighting (HVAC&L) designs.

Low-energy buildings do not always operate as they were designed. Design community professionals rarely go back to see how their buildings perform after they have been constructed. Measurements in all six buildings showed that they used more energy and produced less energy than predicted in the design/ simulation stage.

Information leads to better management and improved performance. Setting and following design goals or traditional commissioning does not guarantee that the goals will be satisfied in actual operations. The whole-building energy performance must be tracked and verified. Monitoring provides valuable feedback that can help maintain the efficient performance of systems to ensure design goals are met.

We can replicate the lessons learned from these case studies in future low-energy buildings. The buildings and the lessons learned from them help to define a set of best practices. Best practices are proven real-world technologies and processes that lead to high-performance buildings. Understanding success and opportunities in the current generation of low energy buildings can improve the energy efficiency of all commercial buildings—the best practices should be applied to future buildings *(Torcellini 2006)*.

vey on "perceptions of building comfort and functionality in the categories of temperature, air quality, lighting, noise, and plumbing fixtures" (Turner 2006).

Actual energy use in the Cascadia case studies was consistently low compared to a comparable "code-minimum" baseline building with an average annual savings of $8 per square foot [$86 per square meter] over a 25-year period. This is consistent with the DOE results and suggests that the energy efficiency measures encouraged by the LEED process do deliver a building that consumes less energy than a standard design. There was, however, little correlation between the actual and *predicted* energy savings based on the energy simulation calculations required by LEED.

Water consumption reports were similar although with less dramatic savings over the baseline. The study authors attributed the disparity between predicted and actual usage for both water and energy to the difficulties in predicting occupant behavior. This is particularly true in the case of water use, which is strongly dependent on individual actions. Building performance prediction tools are clearly necessary to inform the design process, particularly for green buildings, but the Cascadia study results warn against relying too closely on their use to project actual performance.

Another area of research that has been actively pursued over the past five years is the

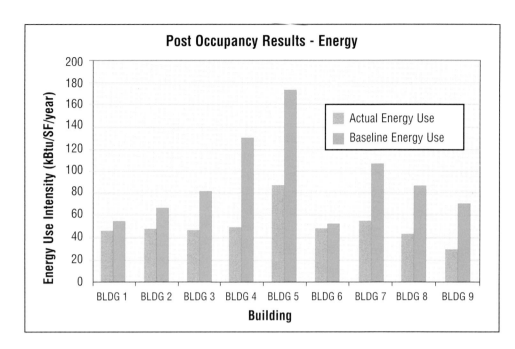

FIGURE 9A
Results from a post occupancy study of green buildings in the Pacific Northwest, comparing actual energy use intensity with a code-minimum baseline. *Source: Cascadia Region Green Building Council.*

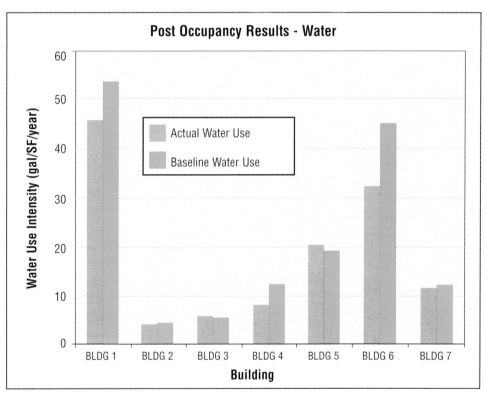

FIGURE 9B
Results from a post occupancy study of green buildings in the Pacific Northwest, comparing actual water use intensity with a code-minimum baseline. *Source: Cascadia Region Green Building Council.*

benefit to human well-being provided by sustainable buildings. It has been a conviction of many green architects that occupants are healthier and more productive in green buildings that feature natural lighting, good ventilation, and air quality, views, and so on. However, the supporting data that has been reported has been thin and anecdotal. Because the potential economic effect of even a small increase in workplace productivity would dwarf the energy cost savings, there is a tremendous interest in research in this area.

BUILDING INVESTMENT DECISION SUPPORT (BIDS™)

Cost-Benefit Tool to Promote High Performance Components, Flexible Infrastructures, and Systems Integration for Sustainable Commercial Buildings and Productive Organizations

1. Daylighting Pays. Maximize the use of daylight without glare and provide daylight-responsive lighting controls to ensure 22-60 percent overall energy savings, 35-65 percent lighting energy savings, and 0.45-40 percent productivity gains, for a return on investment (ROI) over 185 percent.

2. Natural Ventilation Pays. Replace or supplement mechanical ventilation with natural ventilation or mixed-mode conditioning to achieve 47-79 percent HVAC energy savings, 0.8-1.3 percent health cost savings, and 3-18 percent productivity gains, for an average ROI of at least 120 percent.

3. High Performance Equipment Pays. The first trade-off in a "value engineering" exercise is typically to reduce the quality of the equipment and appliances that have been specified. Even short-term energy savings do not seem to be enough to drive decision makers towards quality. Either performance standards or links to productivity, health, and other life-cycle variables will be critical in promoting high performance equipment.

4. Cool Roofs Pay. Replace conventional dark roofs with cool roofing for 2-79 percent cooling energy savings and 14-79 percent peak cooling demand reduction. CMU's BIDS team has identified seven case studies indicating a link between reflective, light-colored roofs and 2.3 percent to 49 percent reductions in annual cooling energy consumption.

5. Task Air Pays (Underfloor Air Systems). Implement underfloor air systems to ensure 5-34 percent annual HVAC energy savings and 67-90 percent annual churn costs savings, for an ROI of at least 115 percent. Twelve studies have shown that UFA systems can pay for themselves in less than one year due to energy, productivity, churn, and facility management benefits.

Carnegie Mellon University Center for Building Performance and Diagnostics (Loftness 2005).

The Cascadia study includes an occupant survey of perceptions of the indoor environmental quality of the case study buildings. Although the number of projects is limited, the results are instructive. The buildings' users reported generally high satisfaction with the overall workspace, indoor air quality, and lighting quality. Temperature satisfaction and acoustic privacy, however, were ranked considerably lower. Since LEED includes a number of credits related to indoor air quality, but only one related to thermal comfort and none related to acoustics, these results may reflect the rating system's emphasis.

In a wider and more comprehensive approach to human performance benefits, the Center for Building Performance and Diagnostics at Carnegie Mellon University (CMU) has surveyed and analyzed hundreds of scientific studies from around the world that investigate the effect of building design on health and/or human performance, as well as building energy consumption. CMU's research has identified a number of occupational health problems as well as worker productivity effects that are caused or exacerbated by poor indoor environmental quality. They have cross-referenced these issues to the design criteria that could help prevent these negative outcomes. The findings are summarized as five key aspects of building design in which the data for significant life-cycle benefits are clear and convincing (Loftness 2005).

In another study of the human benefits from green buildings, the Center for the Built Environment at the University of California, Berkeley has been conducting post occupancy surveys of occupant perceptions of indoor environmental quality in office buildings. The surveys are administered as Internet web-based questionnaires sent to building occupants via e-mail with anonymous responses. A subset of the buildings studied are either LEED-certified or identified as green by the owner or architect. The results of a comparison of the green and "nongreen" offices show that "on average occupants in LEED-rated/ green buildings are more satisfied in … thermal comfort, air quality, cleaning and maintenance, and overall satisfaction with workspace and building" (Abbaszadeh 2006). These results suggest that the focused attention on improved indoor environmental quality in LEED and sustainably designed projects is working.

Similar results have been reported in several other studies, including a small survey by Keen Engineering (now Stantec) of five of their own projects in British Columbia. Their post occupancy evaluations demonstrated that "occupant satisfaction with indoor air quality was consistently higher in the green buildings" (Sanguinetti 2003). And in a detailed case study of a single building, the Herman Miller

SQA building in Holland, MI, designed by William McDonough and Partners, Dr. Judith Heerwagen concludes, "The SQA building clearly lends credence to the "green building hypothesis" … that green buildings are better for people because they generate higher quality, healthier, more habitable spaces than comparable standard-practice buildings" (Heerwagen 2001).

While the reported data is almost uniformly positive on the successes of sustainable design in delivering the kinds of results that are advertised, the scope of the studies is still too limited. More and broader research studies are needed to provide scientifically defensible conclusions. Nonetheless, this ongoing research provides architects with information to focus their design strategies in the most cost-effective areas and offers building owners a valuable guide to better investment in buildings that offer long-term, life-cycle savings as well as benefits to the well-being of their occupants and users.

Cost of Green

Do green buildings cost more? The general consensus seems to be yes, although this begs the question: "more than what?" Many seasoned sustainable design practitioners have maintained that any added costs can be minimized or even eliminated through experience and integrated design. There has been considerable interest in this topic, for obvious reasons, and several recent studies have analyzed construction costs of green buildings. This topic is covered later in detail.

DESIGN PROCESS

A 2005 study by Pennsylvania State University identified the "top three mistakes" found on green building projects that did not meet their goals as:

- Attempting to change a traditional project to a green project mid-stream,
- Treating green building features as add-ons to a building initially designed with traditional values, and
- Poor coordination of energy consultants and considerations for energy use during predesign stages of projects (Riley 2005).

To avoid these mistakes requires a whole-building integrated design approach that front-loads the design process with early interdisciplinary collaboration, conceives of the building as an interactive system of parts that should be designed together, and sets measurable performance goals. The integrated design process is covered later in detail, but the practice implications are summarized here.

An integrated design process frequently includes tasks that are beyond those typically included in standard design services, including the use of advanced computer tools to simulate and predict energy consumption to achieve higher levels of energy efficiency and life-cycle cost savings. Similar "additional" design services include the evaluation of strategies to use natural daylighting to minimize the need for electric illumination, life-cycle costing, and services related to achieving LEED certification.

The integrated design process also addresses issues related to actual building performance and frequently includes more involvement of the design team in the observation of building system installation and start-up through commissioning services. Commissioning provides a closer review of the design intentions of major building systems—mechanical, electrical, and plumbing (MEP), lighting, and controls, for example—and assurance that the building is actually meeting the design and has demonstrated clear benefits and cost savings in building operations. This overlap into building operations is a clear jump over the traditional lines of separation between the designer, builder, and owner, and offers the architect a means to broaden their relationship with the client and a source of valuable feedback on the success of the design.

While these adjustments in design process and project delivery have been easy for some teams and clients, a conscious effort is required. The distribution of work effort in the various design phases is shifted to more high-level collaboration in the beginning. Careful selection of consultants is also important because not all engineering firms have the experience or inclination to join in this type of collaborative process. An adjustment in the scope of services and related compensation is often required.

Many firms are finding that front-loading the design effort in the whole-building integrated design process offers benefits to the project beyond meeting the goals of environmental sustainability. The early collaboration produces a shared understanding of the project and its goals that can produce more coordinated design and documentation in later phases of the design. The inclusion of a commissioning agent in the process has been shown to reduce the problems that arise in the initial period of occupancy as well. While integrated design is most often mentioned in relation to sustainable design, it is in many ways, simply good design.

SUSTAINABLE DESIGN II

PERFORMANCE METRICS FOR SUSTAINABLE DESIGN

The practice of sustainable architecture is clearly expanding and maturing. More clients are asking for green buildings, more firms are claiming green-design expertise, and more manufacturers are advertising green products. But how do we know if we're actually delivering sustainable designs or selecting sustainable products? Because many goals of sustainable design are objective and quantifiable, there are measurable performance assessments that can be used to evaluate the success of these buildings. To date, however, most of these metrics have been obscure and rarely used or discussed within the design and construction industry.

To advance their practice towards sustainability, architects need to become familiar with these key performance yardsticks. Basic performance benchmarks of standard and high-performance building designs can help architects develop a relative sense of achievement for the various measurements. Only by becoming as comfortable and conversant with these metrics as we are with "miles per gallon" or "dollars per square foot" can we design with intelligent and achievable targets for sustainable design.

Measuring architecture using objective criteria may seem heretical to some designers. Design awards rarely ask for performance information, and most professional journals and design magazines do not include such data with the published photos and drawings. Some resistance to the idea of green design by architects can be attributed to an unfamiliarity with using numbers to describe architecture–an endeavor many feel is closer to art than to mathematics.

History provides some insight into the problem of measuring architecture. Vitruvius, for example, assumed his architectural audience had an extensive knowledge of mathematics, geometry, physics, and musical harmonics. He offered many examples of precise measurements of proportions, building plans, plaza layouts, construction machinery, and so on. (His *Ten Books on Architecture* also provide a treatise on sustainable design, including climate-responsive design, proper solar orientation, healthy site selection, use of local materials, and so on. For Vitruvius, this was common-sense design.) A preoccupation with mathematical order in architecture can be found throughout later history, though it is mainly focused on proportional systems of façade composition. Only in the 20th century have measurements of building performance been introduced.

Some building metrics are already in common use. Most experienced architects can estimate the cost of their designs in dollars per square foot or equivalent. Highrise building designers can quote floor area ratios (FAR). Office and school clients often ask about the net-to-gross ratio to express the efficiency of the space layout. These building performance metrics are already in widespread use in the industry. Sustainable design requires that we add a few more key metrics to this list.

References
The basis for most of the metrics described here come from the USGBC's LEED Green Building Rating Systems and the work of the U.S. Department of Energy (DOE) through its Performance Metrics Research

---

PERFORMANCE METRICS FOR SUSTAINABLE DESIGN

Energy
- Energy cost
- Energy use intensity
- Carbon dioxide (CO_2) intensity
- Site vs. source energy use intensity
- Site vs. source CO_2 intensity
- Energy use per household (residential)
- Lighting power density

Water
- Stormwater runoff
- Runoff coefficient
- Water use intensity
- Fixture water consumption per use

Materials
- Life cycle analysis (LCA)
- Building mass
- Percent reused materials
- Percent recycled materials
- Embodied energy
- Embodied CO_2
- Proximity to project site
- Percent renewable

Indoor Air Quality (IAQ)
- CO_2 concentration
- Volatile organic compound (VOC) emissions
- Formaldehyde
- Other toxic emissions
- Thermal comfort
- Lighting/daylighting

Site and Land Use
- Albedo/solar reflectance
- Solar reflectance index (SRI)
- Percent functional ecosystem

Project (Deru and Torcellini 2005) and the Building Cost and Performance Metrics project (Fowler, Solana, and Spees 2005). The LEED Reference Guides along with these publications are invaluable documents for learning about building performance assessment. The DOE work includes metrics for a wide variety of building characteristics. This section draws from those metrics pertaining to a building's environmental performance regarding:

- Energy
- Water
- Materials
- Indoor environmental quality
- Land use and site issues
- Durability

Performance Factors
Building performance is affected by many factors, and not all of them relate directly to design. Climate and other regional differences and variations in project type and building size all affect performance and can make benchmarking and comparisons between buildings difficult. For this reason, many metrics must be *normalized* or converted from absolute values to comparable ratios that facilitate comparison. For example, energy use can be converted from the absolute value of total Btu per year [watts per year] to Btu per square foot per year [watts per square meter per year] to permit a comparison of two buildings of different size. This measure can be further divided by degree-days to allow comparisons between similar buildings in different climates. A degree-day is a characteristic of climate zones and is the difference between the average monthly temperature and 65°F [18.3°C] multiplied by the number of days in the month. There are heating degree-days and cooling degree-days depending on whether the temperature difference is above or below the base temperature.

Human factors during occupancy and operation of a building also have a tremendous effect on performance. For example, daily water consumption in an office building is partially determined by design decisions regarding the type and efficiency of the selected plumbing fixtures. The actual amount of water used, however, is more directly driven by the number of times the occupants flush the toilets, open the faucets, drink from the water fountain, and so on. It is generally easy to determine the efficiency of the fixtures specified for a new building based on the manufacturer's data provided as part of the construction submittal, or from faceplate information on existing equipment. It is very difficult, however, to predict human behavior; assumptions must be made to estimate expected performance. This is one reason there are frequently discrepancies between predicted and actual performance in case studies of built projects.

ENERGY
Buildings use approximately 39 percent of all energy and 71 percent of the electricity produced in the United States (U.S. DOE 2005). The production of energy by the burning of fossil fuels is the single largest source of air and water pollution, including climate-warming CO_2 and other greenhouse gases (GHG).

GHGs are a mixture of CO_2, methane (CH_4), nitrous oxide (N_2O), ozone (O_3), and other trace gases in the atmosphere that absorb terrestrial radiation leaving the surface of the earth. Many are naturally occurring substances, but human activities have altered the equilibrium of these gases. It is generally agreed by the vast majority of scientists that the resulting changes in the atmosphere are having and will continue to have a measurable, potentially calamitous effect on the earth's climate.

Buildings are directly responsible for 43 percent of CO_2 emissions, the most important GHG. This explains why there is a growing interest in the energy efficiency aspects of sustainable design, both in and outside the building industry. This is also why architects have a responsibility to understand how buildings use energy and to learn to design to minimize use of fossil fuels. We also need to understand the patterns of GHG emissions and the environmental impact of other energy sources used in buildings. Learning the metrics used to assess energy consumption and its effects is one key step toward this understanding.

There are a variety of sources providing energy to buildings and many different uses for that energy (figure 10). In buildings, overall energy use is usually measured in either the British thermal unit (Btu) [watt (W)]or the kilowatt-hour (kWh) [megajoule mJ] .

Btus are typically used to measure heating in the United States (although not in Britain!), often delivered by on-site combustion of oil, wood, or gas. Kilowatt-hours are used to measure electricity consumption for lighting, cooling and other equipment. To express total building energy use, either unit can be converted to the other but the most common units are Btu per year [W/year] or kBtu per year [kW/year]. Normalized energy consumption, based on building size, is called the *energy intensity* and is measured in kBtu per square foot per year [kW/m²/year]. The most com-

FIGURE 10

A variety of sources provide energy to buildings, and there are many different uses for that energy. Site energy use refers to the energy that is measured at the building or property line. Source energy use is the energy at the power plant and includes transmission losses and other inefficiencies. *Source: M² Architecture.*

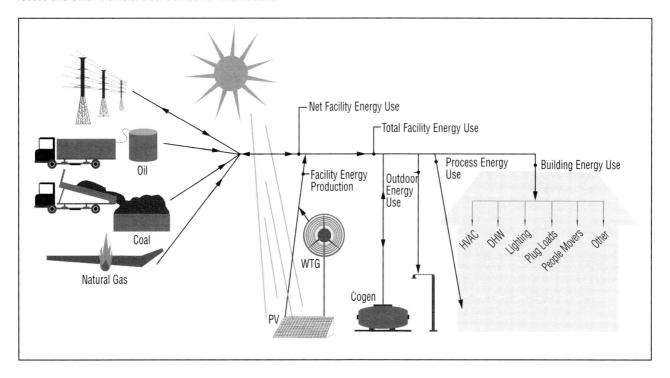

ENERGY STAR

"ENERGY STAR is a joint program of the U.S. Environmental Protection Agency and the U.S. Department of Energy. ENERGY STAR began in 1992 as a voluntary labeling program to identify and promote energy-efficient products to reduce greenhouse gas emissions. Computers and monitors were the first labeled products, but the ENERGY STAR label is now on major appliances, office equipment, lighting, home electronics, and more. EPA has also extended the label to cover new homes and commercial and industrial buildings.

"Through the ENERGY STAR Homes program, builders can achieve an ENERGY STAR label by following design guidelines for insulation, windows, tight construction and ducts, efficient HVAC equipment, lighting and appliances. In addition, a third-party verification by Home Energy Raters includes field testing and inspection. In 2005, 149,568 new ENERGY STAR single-family homes were built, which is nearly 10 percent of all new homes permitted. Through 2005, over 525,000 ENERGY STAR qualified new homes have been built.

"According to EPA (2006), 'More than 2,500 buildings have earned the ENERGY STAR label for superior energy and environmental performance, representing 480 million square feet [44.6 million m^2]. These buildings consume about 40 percent less energy than typical buildings, while providing the required comfort and services. Their owners are saving an estimated $350 million annually on their energy bills relative to typical buildings.'"

ENERGY STAR programs for commercial buildings include a portfolio manager that allows owners to rate the performance of their buildings relative to similar buildings nationwide using EPA's national energy performance rating system. This system accounts for the effects of year-to-year weather variations, as well as building size, location, and several operating characteristics.

Buildings that rate 75 or higher may qualify for the ENERGY STAR. A 75 rating means that the building uses less energy than 75 percent of all similar buildings in the United States. A building with an ENERGY STAR rating of 90 uses less energy than 90 percent of similar buildings.

The ENERGY STAR Target Finder is a useful web-based design tool. Designers provide project zip code, building type, and some basic facility characteristics. The software then calculates an energy intensity target. After the user selects the desired ENERGY STAR rating, the program provides target metrics in energy use intensity, total annual energy use, and total annual energy cost.

Recently added is a measure of how the performance compares to the AIA's 50 percent energy use reduction from an average building of the same use.

At this writing, the program covers the following space types, representing over 50 percent of U.S. commercial floor area:
- Offices (general offices, financial centers, bank branches, and courthouses)
- K-12 Schools
- Hospitals (acute care and children's)
- Hotels and motels
- Medical
- Offices
- Supermarkets
- Residence halls/dormitories
- Warehouses (refrigerated and nonrefrigerated)

Source: EPA ENERGY STAR web site www.energystar.gov

monly used metric for energy is cost and is used as the measure of energy use in the LEED Rating System, for example. Although cost is clearly important to the party paying the energy bills and to the life cycle costing decisions during design, it is a poor indicator of either the pattern of energy consumption or environmental impact.

Overall Building Energy Consumption
Actual building energy use in the United States is tracked in a variety of ways. Usage data is typically tallied separately for commercial, industrial, and residential uses because of the widely varying energy profiles of the buildings from these market sectors. The industrial use is often left out of the building use data due to the difficulty of separating the energy used in building operations from that consumed by industrial processes. Commercial and residential buildings use approximately equal amounts of energy.

The U.S. Energy Information Administration (EIA) publishes detailed data on energy use in existing buildings. Figure 11 lists the average energy intensity and the percentage of total consumption for various types of commercial buildings from 2003. The top three building types for total consumption are offices (19 percent of total commercial energy use), education (14 percent), and health care (10 percent). These rankings for office and education reflect the high number of buildings of these types rather than their relative energy profiles because these are not facilities with high energy intensities. The top three building types for energy intensity are food service (258 kBtu per square foot [756 kWh/m²]), food sales (200) [586] and health care (188) [551]. Such facilities have extensive energy loads related to their internal processes and equipment and would be expected to be very energy intensive.

Residential energy use is normalized into energy intensity per area, as with commercial buildings, but also into energy use by household. Table 1 shows 2001 data for single-family houses, multifamily buildings, and mobile homes. Of the three, single-family houses (the most common type of U.S. housing by far) has the highest total consumption (80 percent of all residential energy use), the highest per household consumption, but the lowest energy intensity (per area).

The EIA data includes all buildings in a given use category—old and new—and reflects the average consumption. Newer buildings, even conventional construction designed using current building codes, have much lower energy intensities and will gradually bring these averages down. Estimates suggest as many as half of all standing buildings in 2050 will have been constructed in the 21ˢᵗ century. Therefore, we need to set ambitious energy targets for new construction, like the AIA's goals, to have a significant impact on overall building energy use. Of course, looked at another way, these estimates mean that nearly half of the buildings that will exist in

FIGURE 11

Energy intensity by building type. *Source: U.S. Energy Information Administration, 2003 Commercial Buildings Energy Consumption Survey.*

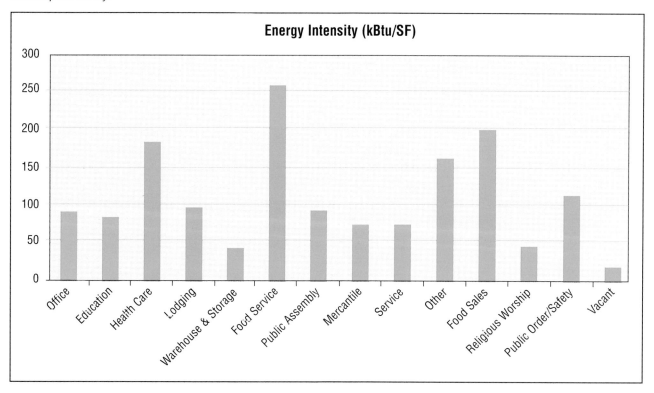

TABLE 1: Residential Delivered Energy Intensities by type (kBtu)

Residential energy use intensities by housing type.
Source: 2006 Building Energy Data Book, U.S. Department of Energy.

Type	per square foot	per household	per household member	percent of total consumption
Single-Family:	44.8	107,300	39,800	80.1%
- Detached	44.7	108,500	39,600	69.4%
- Attached	45.6	100,400	37,500	10.7%
Multi-Family:	52.1	54,300	25,800	14.6%
- 2 to 4 units	56.1	78,100	34,300	7.5%
- 5 or more units	48.5	41,000	20,500	7.1%
Mobile Homes	72.0	75,900	29,400	5.3%

2050 were built in the 20th century or before. Retrofitting and renovating existing buildings to improve energy efficiency is also needed to meet the goals of sustainable design. There is a lot of work to do!

Building Energy Consumption by Function

For design purposes, it is often useful to differentiate between the various uses of energy inside the building. While these can be broken down nearly infinitely, the major ones are:

- Space heating
- Space cooling
- Lighting
- Domestic hot water
- Electronics and computers
- Laundry and cooking (for residential)
- Everything else ("plug loads," people movers, and so on.)

The distribution of energy among these uses varies between different building types. Figure 12 shows a comparison of uses for different building types. In general, the largest energy consumers in residential structures are space heating, water heating, and space cooling. For commercial buildings, lighting is often the largest single use, followed by space heating and cooling. These differences are useful to understand in setting priorities during design. For example, an energy-efficient lighting design is more important in a typical office building than in a typical residence. Investing in a solar hot water system, on the other hand, may make more sense for a house than for a retail building.

Most of these energy uses are measured by the same metrics as overall energy consumption, described above, and vary depending on their source. Space heating is often generated by burning fuel on site and is measured in Btus [W]. The energy used for electrical equipment, such as fans, is measured in kWh [kWh]. There is, however, one other metric, for lighting, that is important to know.

FIGURE 12

Comparison of residential and commercial building energy uses. *Source: 2006 Building Energy Data Book, U.S. Department of Energy.*

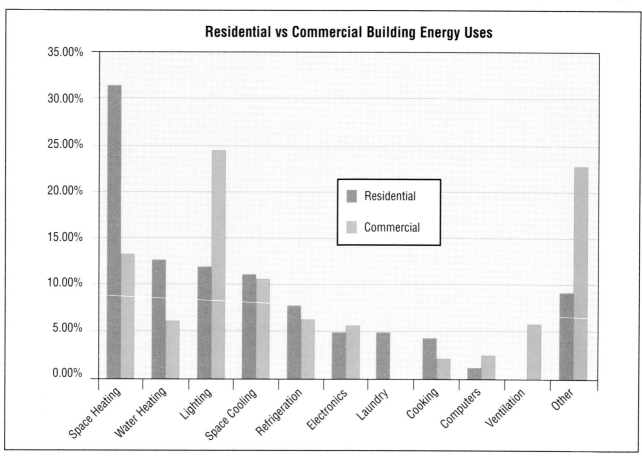

Lighting Power Density

Because lighting is nearly always an electrical load, the related metrics are based on the watt. While lighting consumption is measured in kWh, a lighting design can be expressed as lighting power density (LPD), measured in watts per square foot [W/m^2]. Although the actual energy consumption is also affected by the duration of time the lights are on, which can only be estimated, the LPD is useful as a way to evaluate the efficiency of a lighting design. Energy codes, such as Standard 90.1 of the American Society of Heating Refrigeration and Air Conditioning Engineers (ASHRAE), stipulate maximum LPD figures for either an entire building or by space use type. Table 2 shows typical maximum LPD requirements from ASHRAE 90.1 – 1999 (used as the energy code in many jurisdictions). Also shown in Table 2 is target LPD from the Energy Benchmark for High Performance Buildings v 1.1 (New Buildings Institute 2005). This publication sets prescriptive requirements to achieve an energy-efficient building (10-30 percent better than code) applicable to many building types. The LPD requirements shown here are easily achievable with current technology. Many lighting design professionals will set performance goals even lower than these. Of course, with lighting, quality is as important as quantity. LPD metrics are useful as targets but should not be pursued at the expense of attention to the overall lighting design.

TABLE 2: LIGHTING POWER DENSITIES

Comparison of maximum lighting power densities. *Source: ASHRAE-90.1 and the Energy Benchmark for High Performance Buildings v1.1.*

	ASHRAE 90.1-1999	New Buildings Institute Energy Benchmark
Building Type	maximum W/SF	maximum W/SF
Courthouse	1.4	1.2
Dining: Cafeteria/Fast Food	1.8	1.4
Hospital	1.6	1.2
Library	1.5	1.3
Manufacturing Facility	2.2	1.3
Office	1.3	0.9
Parking Garage	0.3	0.3
School/University	1.5	1.2
Warehouse	1.2	0.6

Zero Energy Buildings

A zero-energy building is generally considered to be one in which annual energy consumption is equal to annual energy production, through on-site renewable energy sources such as solar or wind power. This is also called a *zero net energy building*. DOE's Zero Energy Home program seeks to develop market-ready single family house designs for a variety of climates that have a net-zero energy balance. The cost-effective approach to this goal is as follows:

1. First, minimize the energy load through architectural design with climate-responsive strategies including proper solar orientation and shading, and a tight, well-insulated building envelope,
2. Then use the most efficient mechanical systems,
3. And finally, install renewable energy systems to provide for the remaining energy needs.

With commercial buildings, the approach to achieving zero energy is similar. There are often more opportunities for integrated design approaches in larger buildings as described below.

Environmental Impacts of Energy Consumption

The goals of sustainability are not simply to save energy, but to reduce the negative effects of energy use on the environment. Energy consumption is a strong indicator of ecological impact, and in most cases saving energy means producing less pollution, particularly GHG. However, different energy sources emit different levels of GHG. Other negative effects also vary depending on the energy source. Nuclear power, for example, has little or no impact on climate but can harm adjacent waterways from which the power plants take water for cooling. And, of course, there are serious concerns about the security and safety of the storage of radioactive waste from nuclear plants.

Although CO_2 is not the only greenhouse gas, it is the most prevalent component of GHG and is often used as a single indicator to characterize the impact on climate from an energy source. CO_2 emissions are usually reported in metric tons of carbon (MTC) or million metric tons of carbon (MMTC). An alternate metric that can be used is the global warming potential (GWP). This measures the heat-trapping qualities of an atmospheric gas and is based on the climate-impact characteristics of CO_2. The units of GWP are metric tons of carbon dioxide equivalents ($MTCO_2E$). GWP allows a weighted average comparison of emissions from various sources, taking into account the different mix of gases emitted. Either of these can be normalized to floor area or other building units, as is done with energy metrics, to calculate an emissions intensity, or carbon intensity for buildings. While not yet a metric that is in wide use, carbon intensity may soon become a critical performance benchmark.

Source vs. Site Energy Consumption

Most of the environmental impact of energy use is generated at the source of energy production, typically involving combustion of fossil fuel. This may occur at the building or site, in the case of a natural gas boiler or diesel generator, for example, or the source may be at a distance from the site, in the case of an electrical power plant. Figure 14 shows the CO_2 emissions profile from several common fuels used in buildings.

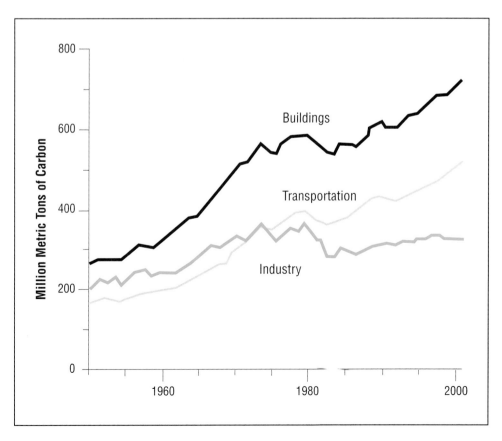

FIGURE 13

Growth in greenhouse gas emissions from buildings, compared to that of industry and transportation. Buildings' contribution to climate change is the largest and fastest growing among these three major sectors of the economy. *Source: Architecture 2030.*

FIGURE 14

Carbon dioxide emissions for various common fuel types. Coal is the most common fuel used to generate electricity in the United States and thus is the largest contributor to greenhouse gases. *Source: 2006 Building Energy Data Book, U.S. Department of Energy.*

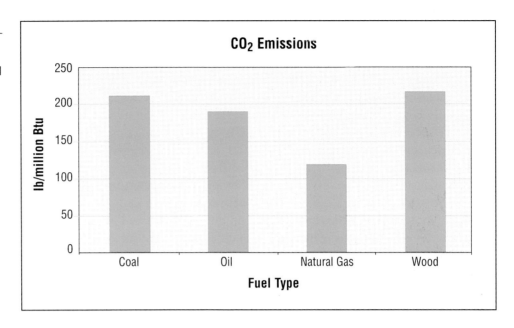

When the source is not within the building, there are inevitably energy losses and inefficiencies during the transmission of the energy from the source to the facility. These losses can be significant, particularly in the case of utility-provided electrical power. In order to properly account for the environmental impacts, like GHG emissions, it is necessary to calculate the energy consumption at the power plant, taking into account the inefficiency of the grid. This is called "source energy" as distinct from "site energy."

Because energy consumption is metered at the building or property line, calculating the source energy from site energy requires some information on the actual energy source and provider. The electrical grid is a network that distributes power from multiple sources in a given region so it is almost never possible to determine the exact plant that supplies a given facility. For this reason, average data is used to convert to source energy, either by utility, by region, or for the country. Table 3 shows average multipliers for different fuel sources.

TABLE 3

U.S. average multipliers for site vs. source energy. A high multiplier indicates a low efficiency of conversion and transmission of energy from the source to the site. *Source: Lawrence Berkeley National Laboratory.*

Fuel Type	Site Energy (kBtu)	Source Energy Multiplier
Electricity	1	3.013
Natural gas	1	1.024
Fuel oil	1	1
Steam	1	1.38

Utilities are required to report their GHG emissions averaged from all of their production facilities. These are frequently reported as pounds of CO_2 or CO_2E per megawatt-hours (lb/MWh) [kG/MWh]. These reports can usually be found on the utility company's web site. There is a wide variation among different utilities and different regions due to the variety of energy sources used. This average emissions output data can be used to convert a building's energy consumption into environmental impact. Of course, if the building user purchases "green power" or uses on-site renewable energy such as photovoltaic panels for a portion of its energy, this will reduce the overall impact, proportionally.

Although site energy use intensity (kBtu per square foot [kWh/m²]) remains a useful metric to compare the design of buildings of similar uses and climate. Source energy is a more accurate reflection of the environmental impacts. For example, two buildings with equal site energy but located in different parts of the country supplied by different utility companies may have very different impact profiles based on source energy.

Carbon Neutral Buildings

Similar to "zero-energy," "carbon-neutral" describes a building that does not increase the amount of GHG in the atmosphere through its construction or operations. A zero-energy building may be carbon neutral, but not necessarily. Zero-

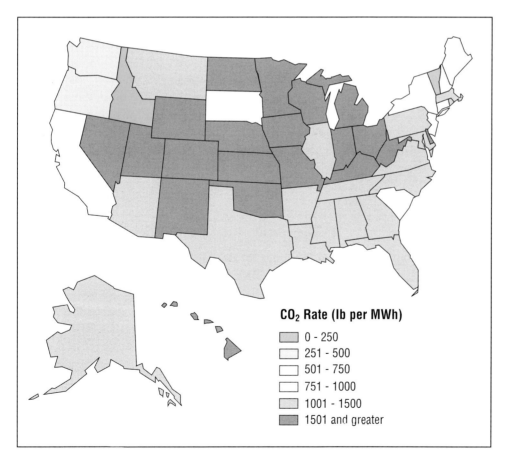

FIGURE 15

Average greenhouse gas emissions by state. *Source: U.S. Environmental Protection Agency.*

CO₂ Rate (lb per MWh)
- 0 - 250
- 251 - 500
- 501 - 750
- 751 - 1000
- 1001 - 1500
- 1501 and greater

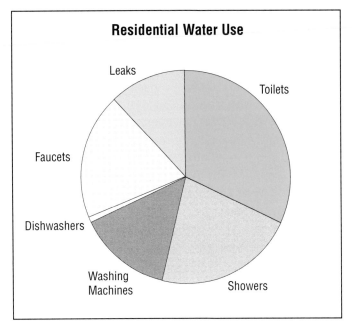

Residential Water Use

energy buildings focus on the operational energy consumption. True carbon neutrality would also look at the "embodied energy," or the energy required to manufacture the products and construct the building, as well as the ongoing energy use. We do not have the ability to easily and practically calculate this data yet, although efforts to develop life cycle analysis tools are underway.

WATER

According to the USGBC LEED v2.2 Reference Guide, buildings account for approximately 25 percent of the water consumption in the country. While not as high as buildings' share of energy use, this is nonetheless significant. Potable water supplies are larger concerns in certain regions than in others, but there is a growing consensus that water scarcity will become a problem across the country. Fortunately, there are considerable opportunities to reduce current levels of water consumption in buildings.

Potable water in urban and suburban areas is usually taken from rivers and other bodies of waters and treated within a municipal infrastructure. Groundwater drawn from wells is still used in rural and less densely populated communities, but only 16 percent of the U.S. population gets its drinking water this way (Hutson et. al. 2005). The environmental effects of water use are different from those of energy. When fuel is converted into energy, the side effects of the conversion are generally negative (pollution, GHG, and so on). With water, however, the impacts are more diverse.

Water is typically used in buildings for drinking, bathing, washing, conveying waste, and as a component of many commercial cooling systems. Potable water is also used outside buildings for irrigation and other maintenance. Much of the "use" of water in and around buildings, then, is actually the conversion of potable water into nonpotable wastewater, which then moves into a waste treatment system, or, in many instances, is discharged into rivers and streams with little or no treatment. According to a 1995 study by the EPA:

> The demand for water in the United States necessitates stream and river impoundments, the drilling of more and deeper wells, and water withdrawals from most natural water bodies across the country. The high

demand for and overuse of water can contribute markedly to nonpoint-source pollution in various forms, including:

- Altered in-stream flows due to surface withdrawals
- Saltwater intrusion due to excessive withdrawals
- Polluted runoff resulting from the excess of water applied for irrigation and landscape maintenance that carries with it sediments, nutrients, salts, and other pollutants
- Other adverse effects result from the damming of rivers to create the large volumes of water in reservoirs. In addition to impacts on natural habitats, dams themselves create several forms of nonpoint source pollution due to their effects on physical and chemical water quality degradation both upstream and downstream.

There are also serious consequences to water being taken from underground aquifers, which may be drawn faster than they can be refilled. The LEED v2.2 Reference Guide states: "In some parts of the United States, water levels in… aquifers have dropped more than 100 feet [30.5 m] since the 1940s. On an annual basis, the water deficit in the United States is currently estimated at about 3,700 billion gallons [14 billion m³]. In other words, Americans extract 3,700 billion gallons [14 billion m³] per year more than they return to the natural water system to recharge aquifers and other water sources."

Site maintenance and landscaping are almost always inappropriate uses for fully treated potable water when lower-quality water, such as graywater, can be substituted Graywater is defined as wastewater from lavatories, showers, bathtubs, washing machines, and sinks that are not used for disposal of hazardous or toxic ingredients or wastes from food preparation. In all cases, the goal for a sustainable design is to minimize the use of potable water.

There are other effects of water on buildings and sites related to rainwater falling on the site or other surface water moving through the site. Significant runoff damage can occur, both to the building site and beyond, due to runoff leaving the site. On an undisturbed natural site, most rainwater soaks into the soil and gradually filters down into the groundwater. When buildings and impervious pavement are constructed, the natural absorption of rain is prevented. The resulting excess stormwater leaves the site as surface runoff and/or captured in manmade structures and conveyed to some downstream body of water. Excess stormwater runoff can cause erosion and degradation of natural streams, loss of topsoil, and downstream water pollution from toxic substances and silt washed from the impervious surfaces. Ecologically sensitive site design includes several *best management practices* that limit excess runoff and encourage groundwater recharge of rainwater within the project property where possible.

Runoff Coefficient

One metric that can be used to characterize the potential of a site or portion of a site to prevent stormwater runoff is the *runoff coefficient*. This measures the share of rain or other stormwater that would be expected to run off a given surface, measured as a fraction of 1.00. A runoff coefficient of 0.95 indicates that most of the water runs off; a surface with a coefficient of 0.05 absorbs most of the stormwater. The runoff coefficient is a function of the surface treatment, use, slope, and underlying soil type. In most cases, recharge is desirable as a stormwater strategy. Therefore, site designs that minimize runoff have low runoff coefficients. Table 4 shows values for typical surface types.

Water Use

The metrics for water consumption and stormwater runoff are based on the volume of water measured in gallons [liters]. The metrics used for potable water consumption are volume per unit of time, such as gallons per month (The Federal Energy Management Program recommended metric) or gallons per year. Water use can be normalized by calculating consumption by area (*water use intensity* in volume per year per area), by number of building occupants, or, for residential, by number of households. There is unfortunately no good water consumption data for commercial buildings using any of these metrics. Table 5 shows typical water consumption data for single family houses in several U.S. cities.

There are a variety of technological and design strategies for reducing the consumption of water in buildings. The current baseline (minimum) water consumption in the LEED Rating System is based on the maximum flow rates for plumbing fixtures established in the Energy Policy Act of 1992. To project water use, one identifies the quantity of fixtures of each type in the building and then makes

FIGURE 17A AND 17B

Impervious surfaces prevent the infiltration of stormwater into the ground leading to surface runoff that harms streams, causes floods, and promotes erosion. Top: the hydrologic cycle for one acre [0.4 hectare] of undeveloped land in the Piedmont area of the eastern United States. Bottom: the effect of development on the same area. *Source: Cahill and Associates.*

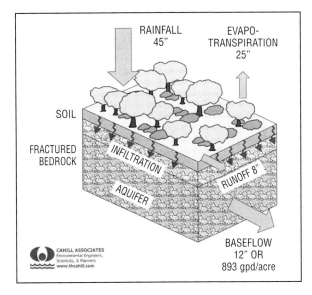

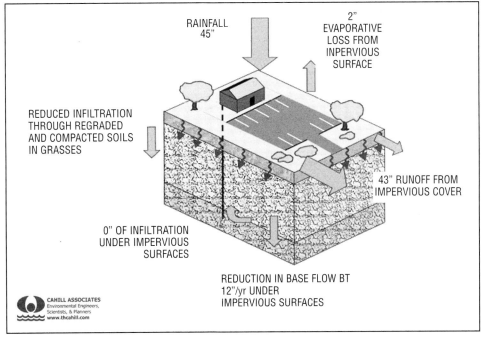

RUNOFF COEFFICIENTS FOR TYPICAL SURFACE CONDITIONS				
SURFACE	Runoff Coefficient		SURFACE	Runoff Coefficient
Pavement, Asphalt	0.95		Turf, Flat (0-1% slope)	0.25
Pavement, Concrete	0.95		Turf, Average (1-3% slope)	0.35
Pavement, Brick	0.85		Turf, Hilly (3-10% slope)	0.40
Pavement, Gravel	0.75		Turf, Steep (> 10% slope)	0.45
Roofs, Conventional	0.95		Vegetation, Flat (0-1% slope)	0.10
Roof, Vegetated Roof (<4 in)	0.50		Vegetation, Average (1-3% slope)	0.20
Roof, Vegetated Roof (4-8 in)	0.30		Vegetation, Hilly (3-10% slope)	0.25
Roof, Vegetated Roof (9-20 in)	0.20		Vegetation, Steep (>10% slope)	0.30

TABLE 4
Runoff coefficients of common surface conditions. *Source: USGBC LEED-New Construction 2.1 Reference Guide.*

	x 1,000 gallons per house per year			%	%
Study Site	Total	Indoor	Outdoor	Indoor	Outdoor
Boulder, CO	134.1	57.4	76.7	42.8%	57.2%
Denver, CO	159.9	64.4	95.5	40.3%	59.7%
Eugene, OR	107.9	63.9	44	59.2%	40.8%
Las Virgenes, CA	301.1	71.6	229.5	23.8%	76.2%
Lompoc, CA	103	62.9	40.1	61.1%	38.9%
Phoenix, AZ	172.4	71.2	101.2	41.3%	58.7%
San Diego, CA	150.1	55.8	94.3	37.2%	62.8%
Scottsdale/Tempe, AZ	184.9	61.9	123	33.5%	66.5%
Seattle, WA	80.1	49.5	30.6	61.8%	38.2%
Tampa, FL	98.9	53.9	45	54.5%	45.5%
Walnut, CA	208.8	75.3	133.5	36.1%	63.9%
Average	**147.6**	**61.8**	**85.8**	**41.9%**	**58.1%**
Standard Deviation	*64.80*	*8.00*	*58.98*		
Coefficient of Variation	*0.44*	*0.13*	*0.69*		
Estimates are based on one year of monthly meter readings. Indoor water use is estimated by averaging water use during the non-irrigation season.					

TABLE 5
Average annual residential water use in 12 U.S. cities. *Source: Heaney et.al.*

assumptions regarding the frequency of use and, where applicable, duration of use of each fixture based on the building occupancy and operations. Because of the highly variable nature of these assumptions, it is difficult to project water use in buildings with any accuracy.

To encourage greater water efficiency, EPA is developing a program called WaterSense, similar to ENERGY STAR, that will rate the water efficiency of plumbing fixtures. According to EPA, "WaterSense will help consumers identify water-efficient products and programs. The WaterSense label will indicate that these products and programs meet water-efficiency and performance criteria." This program will allow architects to more easily identify and specify the top performing water-saving fixtures. (www.epa.gov/watersense)

LIFE CYCLE ASSESSMENT

Life cycle assessment is a composite measure of sustainability that draws on many of the simpler measures presented previously.

"Life Cycle Assessment is a process to evaluate the environmental burdens associated with a product, process, or activity by identifying and quantifying energy and materials used and wastes released to the environment; to assess the impact of those energy and materials used and releases to the environment; and to identify and evaluate opportunities to affect environmental improvements. The assessment includes the entire life cycle of the product, process, or activity, encompassing, extracting and processing raw materials; manufacturing, transportation and distribution; use, reuse, maintenance; recycling, and final disposal."

(Society for Environmental Toxicology and Chemistry 1993)

LCA is the internationally accepted method for evaluating the environmental effects of buildings and their materials. It is a comparative analysis process that evaluates the direct and indirect environmental burdens associated with a product, process, or activity. Life cycle analysis quantifies energy and material use and environmental releases at each stage of a product's life cycle, including:

- resource extraction
- manufacturing
- construction
- service
- postuse disposal

LCA is considered the best tool for these evaluations because it examines the full range of impacts over all the phases of a building's useful life instead of focusing on any particular stage. Considering the cumulative environmental effects over the study period (the assumed service life of the building) allows researchers to make a more complete assessment.

Source: Canadian Architect, (www.canadianarchitect.com/asf/ perspectives_sustainibility/measures_of_sustainablity/ measures_of_sustainablity_lca.htm)

MATERIALS AND WASTE

The construction industry is one of the single largest U.S. users of raw material, accounting for 25 percent of the wood, gravel, and sand used each year and 40 percent of the material flow in the economy. As with energy, the size of the building-material industry is a significant proportion of the overall total, so the environmental impact is substantial. The direct impacts of materials are mainly in their production, known as "upstream" impacts, but there are also negative consequences related to their use, maintenance, and eventual disposal or reuse. These can be substantial and depend on a variety of factors including how and where the raw materials are obtained, the manufacturing processes used, the means of transportation to the site, distance from the site, and so on.

Because of this range of factors, there is no single design metric that can be used to help guide the selection of materials. The process of evaluating all of the various consequences, and weighing the comparisons between the factors, is called life cycle assessment (LCA). In theory, LCA can compare the environmental impacts of different materials or assemblies and provide a "score" that indicates the preferable choices. In practice, LCA is a difficult and complex undertaking requiring extensive data collection and analysis. While there are initiatives underway to develop LCA for building materials in the United States, there is not yet a comprehensive tool that is easily useable in the design process. The National Renewable Energy Lab (NREL) and other federal agencies are developing the U.S. Life-Cycle Inventory (LCI) Database to help LCA experts answer questions about environmental impact. (www.nrel.gov/lci/) The Canadian Athena Institute has an Environmental Impact Estimator (www.athenasmi.ca/index.html).

BEES

The National Institutes of Standards and Technology (NIST) has developed software known as BEES (Building for Environmental and Economic Sustainability) for selecting cost-effective, environmentally preferable building products. BEES is a useful tool for educating architects about LCA, but its data is currently limited to only a few materials. Developed by NIST with support from the EPA's Environmentally Preferable Purchasing Program, BEES is "based on consensus standards and designed to be practical, flexible, and transparent. Version 3.0 of the Windows-based decision support software, aimed at designers, builders, and product manufacturers, includes actual environmental and economic performance data for nearly 200 building products." The BEES software can be downloaded for free from their web site (www.bfrl.nist.gov/oae/bees.html).

The ecological effects that BEES considers are:

- Global warming
- Acidification
- Eutrophication
- Fossil fuel depletion
- Indoor air quality
- Habitat alteration
- Water intake
- Criteria air pollutants
- Human health
- Smog
- Ozone depletion
- Ecological toxicity

This list provides an introduction to the challenges of *weighting*, which designers must confront when making the "apples-to-oranges" comparisons of different types of environmental impacts, requiring subjective judgments as well as objective decisions. BEES users are given a choice of how to weigh the various factors. Because few architects are sufficiently knowledgeable to specify relative importance among the factors, they can opt to use one of several default environmental priority distributions, such as the one established by the EPA Scientific Advisory Board or the weightings from a 1992 Harvard University study. BEES can also include the cost of building products, both "first cost" and life-cycle cost.

BEES can be used to assist architects in comparing the environmental effects of particular products, such as carpet versus vinyl composition tile (VCT) versus linoleum flooring. Although the number of building materials currently available in the software is limited, BEES is continuing to add products and material data. One drawback is the focus on individual products rather than assemblies. BEES can compare brick veneer with aluminum siding, for example, but a better comparison would look at the entire wall assembly because there could be ecologically negative factors at play in the different wall structures, insulations, interior

BUILDING MATERIALS: WHAT MAKES A PRODUCT GREEN?
Summary of Product Standards for GreenSpec

1. Products Made with Salvaged, Recycled, or Agricultural Waste Content
    1a. Salvaged products
    1b. Products with postconsumer recycled content
    1c. Products with preconsumer recycled content
    1d. Products made with agricultural waste material
2. Products That Conserve Natural Resources
    2a. Products that reduce material use
    2b. Products with exceptional durability or low maintenance requirements
    2c. Certified wood products
    2d. Rapidly renewable products
3. Products That Avoid Toxic or Other Emissions
    3a. Natural or minimally processed products
    3b. Alternatives to ozone-depleting substances
    3c. Alternatives to hazardous products
    3d. Products that reduce or eliminate pesticide treatments
    3e. Products that reduce stormwater pollution
    3f. Products that reduce impacts from construction or demolition activities
    3g. Products that reduce pollution or waste from operations
4. Products That Save Energy or Water
    4a. Building components that reduce heating and cooling loads
    4b. Equipment that conserves energy and manages loads
    4c. Renewable energy and fuel cell equipment
    4d. Fixtures and equipment that conserve water
5. Products That Contribute to a Safe, Healthy Built Environment
    5a. Products that do not release significant pollutants into the building
    5b. Products that block the introduction, development, or spread of indoor contaminants
    5c. Products that remove indoor pollutants
    5d. Products that warn occupants of health hazards in the building
    5e. Products that improve light quality
    5f. Products that help noise control
    5g. Products that enhance community well-being

Source: Environmental Building News, January, 2006. (www.buildinggreen.com)

finishes, and so on. However, BEES is useful as an educational tool for understanding the range of environmental harm caused by construction materials.

PROXY METRICS

In the absence of an easily usable, comprehensive LCA tool for material comparisons, the metrics that are available for assessing the environmental impacts of material choices and providing guidance for selection are based on *proxies*. Proxies are selected, individual characteristics that contribute to the overall environmental assessment. These include proportion of salvaged and recycled content, embodied energy, proximity to the project site, renewability, and durability. Information on many of these factors is readily available or can be easily acquired from the manufacturer or supplier for a given material and project. They form the basis of the Materials and Resources criteria of the LEED rating system. The following descriptions of these proxies explains the associated design metrics and how they can be used. The criteria and metrics related to indoor air quality and human health will be covered later.

"REDUCE REUSE RECYCLE"

The 3 R's—a green mantra from way back—represent three approaches to consuming materials in descending order of importance. These can be useful principles thinking about material use in buildings.

Reduce

If we use fewer materials by building smaller structures or designing efficiently and to lessen waste, there are fewer negative consequences. One basic metric might be overall building mass. Buckminster Fuller was known to ask architects, "How much does your building weigh?"(Zung 2001) This is not a measurement that many designers know off the top of their heads, but it is one that can be instructive to calculate. For example, a single-family house weighs between 50 and 60 pounds per square foot [244 – 292 kg/m²], not including foundations, and up to 200 pounds per square foot [976 kg/m²] with the foundation. The mass of a typical 2,200-square-foot [200 m²] house would thus be 60-70 tons [54,000 – 63,000 kg] plus another 100-150 tons [90,000 – 136,000 kg] of foundation. Simply reducing the house's floor area by 10 percent could reduce the impact of the materials accordingly. In light of this, a draft version of the LEED rating system for homes contains a credit that rewards smaller designs and penalizes houses that are larger than average.

Using materials efficiently through smart design is also a strategy to reduce the amount of material and the associated negative effects on the environment. This can be accomplished by reducing structural redundancy and inefficiencies or by incorporating modular products, which minimize cutting and waste during construction. The manufactured housing industry is a model of efficiency in this regard. Because of the factory construction processes and standardized design modules, the waste coming out of a mobile-home plant is very small. Similarly, selecting standard construction-material sizes and modules could result in efficient and "reduced weight" for site-built construction.

In the homebuilding industry, a focus on efficient framing for wood construction can result in a 15-30 percent reduction in wood needed in a typical house (Edminster and Yassa 1998). In commercial construction, similar techniques are being tried. In a dramatic example, the Hearst Tower in New York City, designed by Norman Foster, uses a unique diagonal grid superstructure that required 20 percent less structural steel than a standard design (Pogrebin 2006.) This was recognized as an "Innovation & Design" strategy by the USGBC in the LEED certification for the project. Perhaps Buckminster Fuller's question is not as off-the-wall as it may seem at first.

Reuse

Reusing a material in the form in which it was originally made (salvaging) is an excellent way to limit its environmental impact. As a replacement for a new product, a reused material avoids nearly 100 percent of any negative consequences, depending on how far it must travel to reach the construction site. Although reused materials are not currently a big factor in new construction, local organizations nationwide are developing the infrastructure to receive and distribute salvaged construction products for remodeling and renovation projects. Materials available from these recyclers include lumber, doors, windows, bathroom and kitchen fixtures,

---

WHAT'S IN A HOUSE?

A typical American 1,700-square-foot [160 m²] new house will contain, among other things:

- 9,700 board feet of lumber (33 m²)
- 4,850 square feet of sheathing (451 m²)
- 55 cubic yards of concrete (42 m²)
- 2,518 square feet of siding (230 m²)
- 2,000 square feet of shingles (186 m²)
- 2,500 square feet of insulation ((230 m²)
- 6,484 square feet of drywall (600 m²)
- 300 pounds of nails (136 kg)
- 750 feet of copper wire (230 m)
- 280 feet of copper pipe (85 m)
- 179 feet of plastic pipe (54 m)
- 55 gallons of paint (208 l)

Source: Rocky Mountain Institute, 1995.

FIGURE 18

The headquarters of the Hearst Corporation in New York City, designed by Norman Foster, is the first LEED-certified highrise building. *Source: Hearst Corporation, Michael J. Ficeto, photographer.*

kitchen cabinets, hardware, plumbing, electrical equipment, appliances, and so on. Mostly targeted at the residential market, these organizations frequently combine "deconstruction," or dismantling, operations with a distribution outlet that serves both the wholesale and retail trade. In deconstructing buildings, they carefully, systematically salvage materials for reuse. In parts of the country with a good supply of buildings slated for demolition and high disposal fees, deconstruction can be cost-effective as well as green. Although salvaged building materials are rarely used in commercial construction, there is an active secondary market in used office furniture, particularly systems furniture. The LEED rating systems include credits for using salvaged materials ("Resource Reuse") in the Materials and Resources category. The metric used in LEED is the proportion of reused material to total materials, expressed as a percentage.

Recycle

In general, a recycled product (one that has been reprocessed from recovered instead of virgin material) has less environmental impact than a new one. Recycled content is therefore a useful proxy characteristic for selecting green materials. Manufacturers have used recycled materials in their products for many years, but only recently has this become a desirable feature to be celebrated in brochures and advertisements. The LEED Materials and Resources category awards points for the overall amount of recycled content in building materials. Like resource reuse, this is calculated as a percentage of the total materials that comes from recycled material or "feedstock." There are two kinds of recycled content: "preconsumer" and "postconsumer." Postconsumer content is consumer waste that becomes a raw material for another product and is considered to have a higher "green" value. Preconsumer content is, according to the LEED-CI Reference Guide, "output from a process that has not been part of a consumer product and would otherwise be landfilled, incinerated, or

TABLE 6A

Embodied energy of individual building materials.
Source: Your Home Technical Manual, Commonwealth of Australia (www.greenhouse.gov.au/yourhome/technical/fs31.htm)

MATERIAL	EMBODIED ENERGY (Mj/kg)	MATERIAL	EMBODIED ENERGY (Mj/kg)
Stabilized Earth	0.7	Plywood	10.4
Concrete Blocks	1.5	Glue-laminated Timber	11
Cast-in-Place Concrete	1.9	Laminated Veneer Lumber	11
Precast Tilt-up Concrete	1.9	MDF	11.3
Kiln-Dried Sawn Hardwood	2	Glass	12.7
Clay Bricks	2.5	Imported Dimension Granite	13.9
Gypsum Plaster	2.9	Galvanised Steel	38
Kiln-Dried Sawn Softwood	3.4	Acrylic Paint	61.5
Plasterboard	4.4	PVC	80
Fibre Cement	4.8	Plastics - General	90
Cement	5.6	Copper	100
Local Dimension Granite	5.9	Synthetic Rubber	110
Particleboard	8	Aluminium	170

ASSEMBLY	EMBODIED ENERGY	
	MJ/m²	Btu/SF
WALLS		
Timber frame, wood siding gypsum board interior	188	16,575
Timber frame, clay brick veneer, gypsum board interior finish	561	49,460
Timber frame, aluminum siding, gypsum board interior finish	403	35,530
Steel frame, clay brick veneer, gypsum board interior finish	604	53,251
Cement stabilized rammed earth	376	79,877
FLOORS		
Raised wood framed floor	293	25,832
110 mm concrete slab on ground	645	25,832
200 mm pre-cast concrete T beam/infill	644	56,778
ROOFS		
Timber frame, concrete tile, gypsum board ceiling	251	22,129
Timber frame, terracotta tile, gypsum board ceiling	271	23,893
Timber frame, steel sheet, gypsum board ceiling	330	29,094

TABLE 6B
Embodied energy of construction assemblies. *Source: Your Home Technical Manual, Commonwealth of Australia, www.greenhouse.gov.au/ yourhome/technical/fs31.htm.*

disposed of as waste." Manufacturers can almost always provide data on the percentage of recycled content in their materials or products when requested as part of the required submittal.

Embodied Energy
Embodied energy is any energy required to extract, process, manufacture, or assemble building materials before they arrive at the job site. This can be an important metric because of the serious consequences of energy production. Embodied energy is a major characteristic considered in LCA. Unfortunately, there is little actual embodied energy data available in the United States. Much of the published work on embodied energy is over 30 years old, or from other countries, and is thus of little current use other than for general comparison purposes (Stein 1979). Tables 6a and b show some recent data from Australia showing embodied energy in Btu per pound [kWh/kg] for individual materials and Btu per square foot [kWh/m²] for various construction assemblies.

While embodied energy can be a useful metric for differentiating between materials or assemblies, there are limitations. Fuel source has a significant influence on the environmental effects of energy, but source is not typically captured in embodied-energy data. In addition, operational energy is ignored in these figures. The example of insulation illustrates why this matters. Some insulating materials have a high embodied-energy component but it's not as high as the heating and cooling

TABLE 7

Comparison of the embodied energy—by weight and "insulating unit"— of several common thermal insulation materials. *Source: Environmental Building News.*

MATERIAL	EMBODIED ENERGY IN BTU/LB. (MJ/kg)	EMBODIED ENERGY PER INSULATING UNIT[1] IN BTU (MJ)
Cellulose	750 (1.8)	600 (0.6)
Fiberglass	12,000 (28)	4,550 (4.8)
Mineral Wool	6,500 (15)	2,980 (3.1)
EPS	48,000 (112)	18,000 (19)
Polyisocyanurate	30,000 (70)	14,300 (15)

[1] Insulating unit refers to the mass of insulation required to provide R-20 over one SF at standard density.

energy the insulation saves over the life of the building. Nevertheless, embodied energy data that compares energy input per insulating value can be used to choose between different insulation products.

Proximity to Project Site

One key component of the total embodied energy is the energy used to transport building products and materials to the construction site. This varies for each project and location and is not typically included in the embodied energy data. To determine the impact of the transportation energy would require knowing both how far and by what means the materials come to the site. Table 8 shows the variation in energy required to move one ton of material one mile [kg/km] for different modes of transportation. Such data could be translated into GHG quantities to describe the environmental impact. Unfortunately, it is in practice quite difficult to determine the means of transportation other than the final delivery, which is almost always by truck for most products. Manufacturers and distributors do not yet systematically track transportation mode from factory to distributor.

Given the lack of transportation data, the best substitute metric is simply distance from the factory or other source to the project site. Although this is only an approximation, it can still be used to compare the transportation burden on the environment for those building products. If the final assembly or manufacture of a product is nearby but the raw materials come from farther away, it is important to consider all distance traveled. LEED's Materials and Resources category rewards projects that use materials that are "extracted, processed, and manufactured" within an arbitrarily determined 500-mile distance of the project site. In many parts of the country, it is possible to source most materials within a much smaller region. Paying attention to this metric helps reduce the energy consumed by transportation and also helps support the local or regional economy, an aspect of sustainability that is often forgotten.

TABLE 8

Energy required to transport construction materials. *Source: Environmental Building News.*

Energy Required to Move Materials		
Transport Type	Btu/ton-mile	kJ/tonne-km
Truck	2,946	2,128
Railroad	344	248
Barge	398	287
Ship	170	123

SUSTAINABLE DESIGN II

Renewability

Some building materials, such as wood products, come from biological sources. Sometimes called "bio-based," these natural materials offer many environmental advantages. For example, their development was powered by solar energy (photosynthesis), which is not included in embodied-energy calculations. And they are renewable—they grow back. However, depending on the source of the bio-based material, there can be other, negative environmental effects. For example, wood may come from trees harvested in ways that cause harm to the local ecology. To help identify materials that are more environmentally benign, several initiatives evaluate forestry practices and provide assurance that the selected wood meets these standards.

The most respected standards are developed by the Forest Stewardship Council (FSC), an independent third-party organization that sets guidelines to ensure that wood that comes from forestry "practiced in an environmentally responsible, socially beneficial, and economically viable way" (www.fscus.org). Wood grown on FSC-certified property comes with a "chain of custody" document warranting that the products that arrive on the construction site actually come from that forest. The current metric for LEED credits is the cost of FSC–certified wood measured as a percentage of the cost of all material in the building.

While LEED currently only recognizes certification from the FSC, there are other certification programs active in North America, such as the Sustainability Forestry Initiative (SFI) (www.afandpa.org/). This program was developed by a timber industry group, the American Forest & Paper Association, and is considered by some to be less stringent than FSC. While SFI did not originally require a third-party review of forestry operations as FSC does, it has recently added this requirement, made other revisions, and is gaining respect as a credible source for baseline wood certification (Environmental Building News 2003). The environmental benefits of using wood from all but the most sensitive or illegally harvested forests are great, and either FSC or another respected certification system can help architects avoid the use of wood from the worst sources.

In the past decade, a number of other bio-based materials have been introduced that use agricultural products or even farm waste as the feedstock. Examples of these include particleboard substitutes made from wheat straw, cotton batt insulation, and countertops made from sunflower seed hulls. Like wood products, these bio-based materials are also renewable but can usually be harvested on a more frequent rotation than trees. LEED credits reward the use of these "rapidly renewable" products made from plants that are harvested within a 10-year-or-less cycle. Like certified wood, the metric is the cost of rapidly renewable materials as a percentage of the cost of all the materials in a building. The alternative products that use agricultural waste as feedstock have the added environmental benefit of keeping materials out of the waste stream.

Unfortunately, the farming practices for some of these agricultural materials often consume large quantities of fossil-fuel based fertilizers and toxic chemicals, to the detriment of land and water. These practices may offset the renewability benefits of the products and would, for example, detract from a product's overall LCA score. Sustainable agriculture would reduce these negatives, but there is not yet a comprehensive certification program to ensure the overall environmental benefit of rapidly renewable materials.

INDOOR AIR QUALITY

Over the past decade, scientific studies have investigated the effects of IAQ on the health and productivity of human occupants in buildings. Taken together, the evidence is very strong that improved IAQ has been linked to better health, higher productivity, and other positive outcomes. While many characteristics of the indoor environment are known to affect humans, only a few are directly related to building design and material selection. The design-related factors most frequently used as indicators for evaluating IAQ are:

- CO_2 concentrations
- VOC emissions
- Formaldehyde
- Other toxic chemical emissions
- Humidity and moisture
- Thermal comfort
- Lighting quality/daylighting
- Views
- Mold and mildew
- Ventilation rate

CO_2 Concentrations

Carbon dioxide is a naturally occurring gas produced by a number of common processes, including human respiration. In HVAC system and building design, CO_2 concentration can be used as an indicator of the effectiveness of ventilation, particularly in densely occupied spaces such as assembly spaces, conference areas, and classrooms. The metric for CO_2 is the concentration, expressed in parts of CO_2 per million parts of air (ppm). Outdoor levels vary between 300 and 500 ppm, depending on location, and have been increasing dramatically over the past century. When indoor CO_2 concentration rises above 1000 ppm, occupants may describe the air as "stuffy" and become drowsy. The specification and use of CO_2 monitors to help control ventilation is one easy and relatively inexpensive way to ensure adequate fresh air. One thousand ppm is a standard maximum level for these controls, but it is worth noting that the EPA campus in Research Triangle Park, NC established a maximum indoor CO_2 level of 800 ppm.

VOC emissions

Volatile organic compounds (VOCs) are carbon-based gases emitted by a variety of materials and products found or used in interiors. These include paints and lacquers, paint strippers, cleaning supplies, pesticides, building finish materials, and furnishings. According to the EPA, "VOCs include a variety of chemicals, some of which may have short- and long-term adverse health effects. Concentrations of many VOCs are consistently higher indoors (up to ten times higher) than outdoors." (www.epa.gov/iaq/voc.html)

VOC metrics are expressed as grams per liter (g/L). While there are no federal standards, VOCs in some products are regulated by local jurisdictions. Manufacturers are required to report their concentration levels. Several organizations provide guidelines for acceptable VOC levels for different types of products, and the LEED Green Building Rating System refers to some of these. For the "Low-Emitting Materials" credit, EQ 4.1 and 4.2, the LEED standards are the maximum VOC lim-

SUSTAINABLE DESIGN II

TABLE 9

Sources and potential health effects of indoor air pollutants. *Source: California Air Resources Board, (www.arb.ca.gov/).*

Sources and Potential Health Effects of Indoor Air Pollutants		
Pollutant	**Major Indoor Sources**	**Potential Health Effects***
Environmental Tobacco Smoke	Cigarettes, cigars, and pipes	Respiratory irritation, bronchitis and pneumonia in children, emphysema, lung cancer, and heart disease
Carbon Monoxide	Unvented or malfunctioning gas appliances, wood stoves, and tobacco smoke	Headache; nausea; angina; impaired vision and mental functioning; fatal at high concentrations
Nitrogen Oxides	Unvented or malfunctioning gas appliances	Eye, nose, and throat irritation; increased respiratory infections in children
Organic Chemicals	Aerosol sprays, solvents, glues, cleaning agents, pesticides, paints, moth repellents, air fresheners, drycleaned clothing, and treated water	Eye, nose, and throat irritation; headaches; loss of coordination; damage to liver, kidney and brain; various types of cancer
Formaldehyde	Pressed wood products such as plywood and particleboard; furnishings; wallpaper; durable press fabrics	Eye, nose, and throat irritation; headache; allergic reactions; cancer
Respirable Particles	Cigarettes, wood stoves, fireplaces, aerosol sprays, and house dust	Eye, nose and throat irritation; increased susceptibility to respiratory infections and bronchitis; lung cancer
Biological Agents (Bacteria, Viruses, Fungi, Animal Dander, Mites)	House dust; pets; bedding; poorly maintained air conditioners, humidifiers and dehumidifiers; wet or moist structures; furnishings	Allergic reactions; asthma; eye, nose, and throat irritation; humidifier fever, influenza, and other infectious diseases
Asbestos	Damaged or deteriorating insulation, fireproofing, and acoustical materials	Asbestosis, lung cancer, mesothelioma, and other cancers
Lead	Sanding or open-flame burning of lead paint; house dust	Nerve and brain damage, particularly in children; anemia; kidney damage; growth retardation
Radon	Soil under buildings, some earth-derived construction materials, and groundwater	Lung cancer
*Depends on factors such as the amount of pollutant inhaled, the duration of exposure and susceptibility of the individual exposed		

its from the California South Coast Air Quality Management District (SCAQMD) for indoor adhesives, sealants, clear wood finishes, stains, and floor coating. Similarly, LEED adopts the Green Seal Standard for Commercial Adhesives (GS-36) for spray-applied (aerosol) adhesives and paints. For carpet VOC emissions, LEED refers to the Carpet and Rug Institute (CRI) Green Label Plus test. The use of carpets that meet this threshold are awarded points under LEED EQ credit 4.3.

Formaldehyde

Formaldehyde is a chemical found in many building materials, including the resins used to manufacture particleboard and other composite wood panel products. Phenol formaldehyde resins are typically used in exterior plywood; they emit less

TABLE 10

Volatile organic compound (VOC) limits for LEED for New Construction Materials & Resources Credit 4.2: "Low Emitting Materials, Paints and Coatings." *Source: USGBC LEED for New Construction 2.2 Reference Guide.*

Volatile Organic Compound (VOC) Limits for LEED – New Construction Materials & Resources Credit 4.2 Low Emitting materials – Paints and Coatings		
Paint or Coating Type	**Maximum VOC content (grams per liter)**	
Architectural paints, coatings and primers	Flats:	50 g/L
	Non-Flats:	150 g/L
Anti-corrosive and anti-rust paints		250 g/L
Clear wood finishes: varnish 350 g/L; lacquer		550 g/L
Floor coatings		100 g/L
Shellacs: clear		730 g/L
Shellacs: pigmented		550 g/L
Stains		250 g/L

formaldehyde than the urea formaldehyde resins used in indoor products. Formaldehyde is naturally present at low levels in both outdoor and indoor air. When present in the air at higher concentrations, occupants experience, according to the National Safety Council's Environmental Health Center, "acute health effects including watery eyes; burning sensations in the eyes, nose, and throat; nausea; coughing; chest tightness; wheezing; skin rashes; and other irritating effects." (www.nsc.org/ehc/indoor/formald.htm)

Formaldehyde concentrations are measured in ppm of air. Urea formaldehyde in plywood and particleboard used in manufactured housing has been regulated by the U.S. Department of Housing and Urban Development (HUD) since 1985 because of a history of IAQ problems in that industry. HUD requires special testing of these products and specifies a maximum concentration of formaldehyde for wood products used in mobile homes. LEED provides a credit for projects that use no composite wood or agrifiber materials with urea formaldehyde resins. The World Health Organization recommends that indoor exposure to formaldehyde should not exceed 0.05 ppm. Minimizing the interior use of materials that contain urea-formaldehyde is recommended.

Other toxic chemical emissions

CO_2, formaldehyde, and VOCs are the main indoor air gases measured in assessing IAQ, but they are by no means the only chemicals of concern. In fact, in California's Section 01350 Special Environmental Requirements, applied to all state-funded projects, lists over 70 toxic "chemicals of concern" along with maximum concentration levels that are permitted in building materials (www.chps.net/manual/documents/Sec_01350.doc). These requirements can be referenced or excerpted in an architect's project specifications. A list of materials that meet Section 01350 requirements can be found on the California Integrated Waste Management Board (CIWMB) web site (www.ciwmb.ca.gov/greenbuilding/Specs/Section01350/#Model_Specifications).

Other states and organizations have developed similar screening mechanisms for product emissions. The Greenguard Environmental Institute has developed a certification program for interior building materials that meet a variety of thresholds for emissions, including those required by Washington state's indoor air quality program for new construction, EPA procurement specifications, and the recommendations from the World Health Organization. A list of products that have been certified are listed on the Greenguard web site (www.greenguard.org). LEED for Commercial Interiors (LEED-CI) recognizes this certification for systems furniture and seating in EQ Credit 4.5. Alternatively, furniture for which tested emissions are below set thresholds for four specific classes of chemical contaminants—Total VOCs (TVOC), formaldehyde, total Aldehydes, and 4-PC—also meet the requirements of this LEED-CI credit.

Thermal Comfort

What is the most common complaint from building occupants? *I'm too cold.* What is the second most common complaint? *I'm too hot.*

Thermal comfort is one of the most immediate and direct human sensations and so is important in the overall, perceived indoor environmental quality (IEQ). The metrics for thermal comfort (psychrometrics) are well established in mechanical engineering standards such as those published by ASHRAE and will not be repeated here. It is highly recommended that architects consult with both the mechanical engineer and the client to come to an agreement on targets for thermal comfort ranges as a basis for design. Thermal criteria can significantly affect energy consumption and HVAC system sizing. Clients often find that relaxing their comfort requirements a little can yield big savings in both initial and life-cycle costs.

Lighting Quality/Daylighting

Recent studies have demonstrated strong correlations between effectively daylit interiors and increased productivity in workplaces and classrooms. Similar results have been shown for high-quality lighting in general. However, it is difficult to measure illumination quality, and often quantity is the only metric used in designing a lighting system. The Illumination Engineering Society of North America (IESNA) establishes standards for light levels for different uses, measured in footcandles (fc). However, lighting quality is determined by characteristics other than footcandle levels, including contrast, glare, and color, which can be difficult to quantify.

Daylighting is also difficult to measure, but there are some useful metrics to help guide design. The key metric is glazing factor, sometimes called daylight factor. The glazing factor is defined as "the ratio of interior illuminance at a given point on a given plane (usually the workplane) to the exterior illuminance under known overcast sky conditions." In other words, this is a measure of how much of the available exterior daylight is transmitted to a work surface. The glazing factor is a function of size and geometry of the room and the area, configuration, and transmissivity of the glazing system. A glazing factor of 2 percent for 75 percent of the occupied space is the threshold for achieving credit for daylighting in LEED.

SITE AND LAND USE

Most of the environmental impacts and metrics discussed so far have involved regional or global problems such as climate change and water pollution. Construction also causes site-specific harm to the ecosystem immediately surrounding the building, through stormwater runoff, production of heat islands, and disruption of wetlands or natural habitat. Because ecological systems are complex, any harm done to them is difficult to measure in simple metrics that might be useful for architects. So, as with materials, we use proxy metrics to help guide design decisions.

The "heat island effect" occurs in densely developed areas where dark-colored pavements and building surfaces absorb solar radiation and reradiate heat, causing an increase in the surrounding air temperature. This rise in temperature prompts air conditioners to work harder, exacerbating air quality problems. The design metrics for this situation are the specific characteristics of paving and roofing materials that affect their contribution to heat islands. The two relevant measurements are solar reflectance, or albedo, the ratio of reflected radiation divided by incoming radiation, and emissivity, a measure of a material's ability to emit radiation. Highly reflective materials contribute less to the heat island because they absorb less solar radiation. Those with lower emissivity are better because any solar heat that is absorbed is not easily reradiated. Combining the two characteristics into a single metric yields the solar reflectance index (SRI). LEED rewards paving and roofing that exceed a minimum SRI in Sustainable Sites credit 8.

Solar reflectance index (SRI) for standard paving materials. *Source: USGBC LEED for New Construction 2.2 Reference Guide.*

Solar Reflectance Index (SRI) for Standard Paving Materials			
Material	**Emissivity**	**Reflectance**	**SRI**
Typical New Gray Concrete	0.9	0.35	35
Typical Weathered* Gray Concrete	0.9	0.20	19
Typical New White Concrete	0.9	0.7	86
Typical Weathered* White Concrete	0.9	0.4	45
New Asphalt	0.9	.05	0
Weathered Asphalt	0.9	.10	6

*Reflectance of surfaces can be maintained with cleaning. Typical pressure washing of cementitious materials can restore reflectance close to original value. Weathered values are based on no cleaning.

Disruption of site ecosystems, habitat, wetlands, and other natural systems is often a consequence of construction activities, particularly on undeveloped "greenfield" sites. Determining the level and the significance of this disturbance requires the work of ecologists and other biologists. This intensity of investigation is sometimes required, particularly on large, government-funded projects calling for environmental impact reports. On most smaller projects, it is not feasible to employ scientific services. There is no direct metric for characterizing ecosystem disturbance, but the AIA's Top Ten Awards program has identified a simple metric that can be applied as a macro-level indicator of site disturbance—the proportion of the site that functions as an on-site ecosystem. This is defined as:

SUSTAINABLE DESIGN II

Landscaped open spaces, urban plazas, bioswales, vegetated rooftops, etc. that are predominantly self-maintaining, and may provide passive cooling, shading, and wind protection. The area defined as an ecosystem must accomplish the following at a minimum: stormwater filtration, groundwater recharge, and habitat for native plants and animals.

Although this metric may at first seem applicable only in rural, open areas, it can also be used in dense suburban or even urban sites. It is possible to have a more functional ecosystem than a standard mowed grass yard by specifying native plantings, stormwater recharge, and other strategies that provide a more diverse habitat. Roof gardens can provide habitat for insects and birds, even on top of urban highrise buildings.

FIGURE 19

The site and building design of this addition to the Sidwell Friends School in Washington, DC, work together to provide a functioning on-site ecosystem. The terrace-constructed wetlands will treat the building's stormwater and wastewater, provide habitat, and serve as an integral part of the curriculum. *Rendering by Kieran Timberlake Associates and Andropogon Associates.*

DRAWING BY ANDROPOGON ASSOCIATES LTD AND KIERAN TIMBERLAKE ASSOCIATES

1. EXISTING MIDDLE SCHOOL
2. MIDDLE SCHOOL ADDITION
3. TRICKLE FILTER WITH INTERPRETIVE DISPLAY
4. WETLANDS FOR WASTEWATER TREATMENT
5. RAIN GARDEN
6. POND

FIGURE 20

Vegetated or "green" roofs are effective in managing stormwater, particularly in urban areas. This green roof is on the Oaklyn Library in Evansville, IN. *Design by VPS Architecture in association with Engberg Anderson, photography by Jerry Butts.*

FIGURE 21

The exuberant front yard in Philadelphia, designed by Tavis Dockwiller of Viridian Landscape Studio, replaced a standard lawn with native plants and a naturalistic aesthetic that provides habitat for a wide variety of organisms. *Source: Tavis Dockwiller.*

Using the Metrics

This long list of metrics is not intended to be comprehensive in assessing a building's environmental performance, or to take the place of a building rating system. The metrics are, however, meant to describe objective measurements that can help guide architects in the design process and expand our common understanding of environmental performance.

SUSTAINABLE DESIGN II

BUILDING RATING SYSTEMS

WHY DO WE NEED RATING SYSTEMS?

Before 1998, when the LEED Green Building Rating System was first introduced, there was no standard or commonly accepted definition of a "green" building in the United States. There were certainly buildings being designed to address environmental issues. Some of these projects focused on energy efficiency, others featured lots of recycled or other green materials, many were concerned primarily with occupant health, while still others tried to integrate the building design into the landscape. Each of these was considered to be a "green building" or a "sustainable design." Without a shared understanding of how the various design strategies might be combined into a balanced, comprehensive approach, there was no way to compare the different buildings or to provide guidance on what was and was not green.

Along with a clear need for a shared definition of green building, architects were looking for help translating the goals of sustainability into design criteria. Because these goals are based on an evaluation of environmental performance, there was also an implicit need to assess the expected performance of the design and judge its level of success at achieving the desired goals. Given the broad scope of the sustainability agenda, architects needed a way to organize this long list of criteria for green design. Which are most important? How do we compare dissimilar goals?

Beyond the design community, building owners who wanted to incorporate their own goals for environmental responsibility into their capital projects were also looking for a tool to help them evaluate designs (and designers) and assist in their own facility-related decision making. At the same time, government agencies promoting environmental sustainability had recognized the influence of the building industry and wanted a way to encourage less damaging construction and development strategies. While still an evolving tool, it is fair to say that LEED has accomplished some of these goals but not yet all of them.

LEED

LEED was developed by the USGBC in the mid-1990s and was modeled partly on the British Research Establishment Environmental Assessment Method (BREEAM) developed in Great Britain, although with some significant differences. BREEAM is a performance assessment method based on actual building data, and it requires that the building be completed and operating for at least a year. In addition to providing a building rating system, LEED was designed as a "market transformation" tool to jumpstart the greening of the U.S. architecture and construction industry, which was only just beginning to be aware of the concept of sustainable design. For this reason, and perhaps as a reflection of the impatient nature of U.S. culture, LEED focuses on design, and a building can receive a LEED certification as soon as it is constructed.

What is LEED?

At its core, LEED is a tool for recognizing and rewarding advanced environmental performance in buildings through a certification process run by the USGBC. Each of several versions is divided into categories of environmental impact that are further divided into subcategories known as "credits." Points are earned towards a LEED rating by designing and/or operating the building to meet the requirements of the various credits, some of which are required ("prerequisites") while others are optional.

Each credit represents a particular environmental performance goal or benefit. Most require the project's design or operations to demonstrate performance beyond that of a "typical" project of similar size, type, and location. For example, in LEED for New Construction, the "Optimize Energy Performance" credit requires calculations of the anticipated annual energy cost and the savings compared to a building designed to meet the requirements of ASHRAE Standard 90.1 (see figure 22B). A 10.5-percent reduction earns 1 point, a 14-percent reduction earns 2 points, and so on up to 10 points for a 42-percent improvement. Other credits require a signed statement from the appropriate team member that the project meets the credit requirements. The LEED for Commercial Interiors (LEED-CI) credit called "Low Emitting Materials: Systems Furniture and Seating" requires a statement "signed by the architect, interior designer, or responsible party, declaring that all systems furniture and seating" meet one of two tests for chemical contaminant emissions. (www.usgbc.org)

If a minimum percentage of the optional points are achieved, along with the prerequisites, the project qualifies to be "LEED Certified." As more points are earned above this basic level, there is a sliding scale of certification levels from Silver to Gold

FIGURE 22A

The LEED "scorecard" lists all the credits and associated points that can be achieved in the rating system and can be used to track the status of the anticipated LEED rating through each phase of a project. *Source: USGBC.*

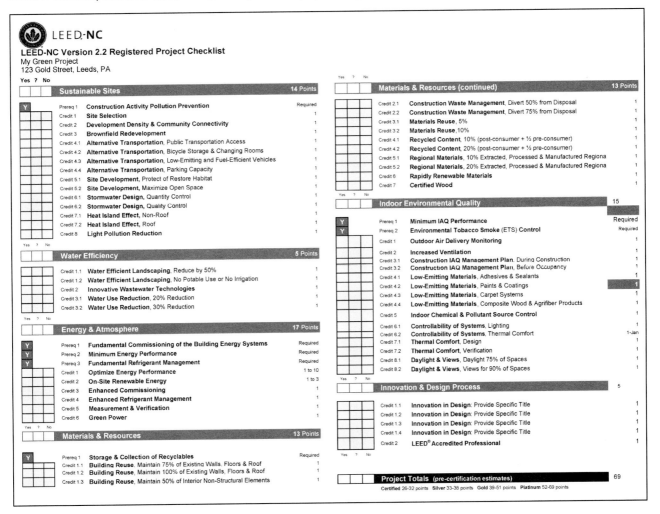

to the ultimate, Platinum. The process of achieving certification requires an initial registration with the USGBC, which then provides access to various on-line resources for the project team. During the design and construction phases, the team gathers the required submittals and documentation. Once the building is completed and occupied, the final certification application and supporting documentation is submitted through the USGBC web site. The Council reviews the application and may request additional clarification or information. Once all required data is received and approved, the project receives its certification, including a LEED plaque (figure 23) and a listing on the web site.

EA CREDIT 1: OPTIMIZE ENERGY PERFORMANCE
1-10 POINTS

Intent
Achieve increasing levels of energy performance above the baseline in the prerequisite standard to reduce environmental and economic impacts associated with excessive energy use.

Requirements
Select one of the three compliance path options described below. Project teams documenting achievement using any of the three options are assumed to be in compliance with EA Prerequisite 2.

OPTION 1 — WHOLE BUILDING ENERGY SIMULATION (1-10 Points) Demonstrate a percentage improvement in the proposed building performance rating compared to the baseline building performance rating per ASHRAE/IESNA Standard 90.1-2004 (without amendments) by a whole building project simulation using the Building Performance Rating Method in Appendix G of the Standard. The minimum energy cost savings percentage for each point threshold is as follows:

New Buildings	Existing Building Renovations	Points
10.5%	3.5%	1
14%	7%	2
17.5%	10.5%	3
21%	14%	4
24.5%	17.5%	5
28%	21%	6
31.5%	24.5%	7
35%	28%	8
38.5%	31.5%	9
42%	35%	10

FIGURE 22B
Each LEED credit is documented with the intent that describes the environmental, health, or other benefit that the credit is intended to achieve. The requirements section describes the measurable action that must be demonstrated in the project to show compliance with the credit. *Source: USGBC.*

LEED was conceived as a voluntary, market-driven rating system. USGBC believes strongly that the life cycle economics along with the positive health and productivity impacts of green buildings are sufficiently compelling that the market will adopt them on their own. As noted above, there is evidence that this is beginning to happen in certain market sectors. Notwithstanding the "voluntary" intention of its originators, LEED has been adopted as a required minimum standard by a number of cities, states, and federal agencies for their own self-funded projects. One of the main reasons for this is the "third-party verification" component of the certification. When a project earns a LEED certification, it is no longer just the architect, builder, or owner claiming that a building is green. Agencies and institutions frequently rely on such third-party standards to provide additional credibility and oversight. For these same reasons, LEED certification has become a condition for a variety of incentive programs, including tax credits and rebates.

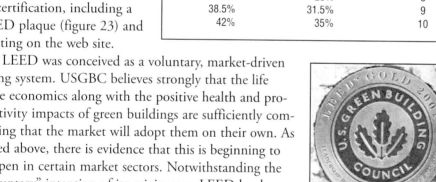

FIGURE 23
LEED plaques are awarded to certified projects. *Source: USGBC.*

While the LEED Rating System is intended for projects and teams that intend to pursue the third-party certification through the USGBC process, many project teams use LEED informally as a design guide or checklist, particularly when there is no LEED requirement from the client or a tax credit or similar incentive. This can be a way for projects with less ambitious goals to address environmental performance yet avoid some of the costs associated with full certification, such as the fees paid to the USGBC and for services required to organize, assemble, and submit the LEED documentation. However, most experienced professionals believe there are benefits to going through the formal LEED process. If the entire design, construction, and owner team are committed to achieving certification, there is much less chance that the inevitable changes and substitutions that occur on any construction project will jeopardize the environmental performance required for LEED. In other words, LEED certification can help ensure that the client will get the actual green building that was designed. The LEED plaque is a good indication that the building delivers improved environmental performance.

The USGBC is a volunteer-driven organization, and the development and ongoing revisions to LEED are mainly accomplished with volunteers in a relatively open and transparent process. (The USGBC has applied for approval as an American National Standards Institute (ANSI) standard-producing organization.) The main framework of LEED is continually evolving. The original version was written for office and highrise residential buildings, but was immediately used on a variety of project types. It soon became apparent that there were difficulties in applying LEED to building types with unique requirements, such as hospitals and laboratories. Reflecting the membership-driven consensus basis of the USGBC, several committees were formed to adapt LEED to these specific building types.

The original version is now called LEED for New Construction (LEED-NC) and remains the flagship product. Figure 24 shows the other versions of LEED that have been or are in the process of being developed to address specific needs of the building industry. USGBC provides guidelines for deciding which version to use for different project types, but more than one LEED rating system may be suitable for a particular project. There are no restrictions other than the project's ability to meet the prerequisites in each LEED category. USGBC "encourages the project team to tally a potential point total using the rating system checklists for all possibilities."

FIGURE 24

LEED for New Construction is the original version of the rating system, but there are now several versions of the LEED Rating System targeted to different project types. *Source: USGBC.*

LEED for New Construction

LEED-NC is the descendant of the original version of the rating system and remains the most widely used. Though originally targeted at new commercial office buildings, it can be used on any type of commercial occupancy and for residential structures above four stories. LEED-NC is ideally suited for new construction or for major renovations. The key criteria for its use for an existing building project are a substantial upgrade to the HVAC and lighting systems to achieve energy efficiency, substantial building envelope modifications, and major interior renovations. While those renovations are not required in a existing building seeking LEED-NC certification, it is, in practice, difficult or impossible to achieve a sufficient number of credits if these components are not being replaced.

LEED-NC is divided into five major categories, reflecting separate areas of environmental and health concerns:

- Sustainable sites
- Water efficiency
- Energy and atmosphere
- Materials and resources
- Indoor environmental quality

There is a sixth category, called "Innovation in Design" that serves as a sort of wild-card section for exemplary or unique approaches.

While LEED-NC has been applied to a wide variety of building and project types, it still reflects its original focus on office buildings in some of its requirements. For example, there is a credit for providing views from inside the building to a majority of building users because there is data suggesting that views of nature provide productivity and health benefits to workers in office buildings. Achieving this credit can lead to workspace layouts that are different from those of typical office buildings. However, in a highrise residential building, for example, this credit is achieved automatically by a code-compliant design. In other project types that use LEED-NC, such as retail stores, the benefits providing views for occupants are somewhat less clear.

One of the most common mistakes made on potentially sustainable projects is waiting too long to decide to "go green." Committing to pursuing LEED certification at the beginning of a project can help teams set performance goals and provide the metrics to assess their success at achieving these goals. This goal setting and continual assessment is an important part of the integrated design process, described in detail later. As an example, if one of the project goals is water conservation, the team might commit to achieving 4 of the 5 possible points in the Water Efficiency category. During schematic design, the team would explore options to use less potable water such as specifying low-flow plumbing fixtures, or using captured rainwater from the roof to flush toilets, or perhaps adopting an innovative on-site wastewater treatment from which the effluent could also be used for flushing. The various strategies would be evaluated for cost, performance, acceptability to the client and users, and other factors. As decisions are made and the design is developed through each phase of design, the effect on the LEED score is reviewed. This iterative process ensures that the individual performance metrics—as well as the overall project goals—are achieved by the design. At the completion of construction documentation, an anticipated LEED score and certification level can be calculated.

Once the project goes into construction, the expected LEED rating serves as a guidepost. While some LEED-NC credits are based solely on the project design, such as those related to site selection or the provision of facilities to manage recyclables, others require verification or submittals generated during construction, such as the amount of construction waste recycled or the cost of recycled materials used. During construction, the builder has a significant role in LEED projects and must understand the process and the documentation for which he or she is responsible.

POST CONSTRUCTION CREDITS

The following credits from LEED for New Construction are "Construction Credits" and can only be submitted after construction has been completed. All other credits can be submitted after construction documents are complete:

SSp1	Erosion and Sedimentation Control
SSc5.1	Reduced Site Disturbance, Protect or Restore Open Space
SSc7.1	Heat Island Effect, Non-Roof
EAp1	Fundamental Building Systems Commissioning
EAc3	Enhanced Commissioning
EAc5	Measurement & Verification
EAc6	Green Power
MRc1.1	Building Reuse, Maintain 75 percent of Existing Shell
MRc1.2	Building Reuse, Maintain 100 percent of Existing Shell
MRc1.3	Building Reuse, Maintain 100 percent of Existing Shell and of 50 percent Non-Shell
MRc2.1	Construction Waste Management, Divert 50 percent from Landfill
MRc2.2	Construction Waste Management, Divert 75 percent from Landfill
MRc3.1	Resource Reuse, 5 percent
MRc3.2	Resource Reuse, 10 percent
MRc4.1	Recycled Content, 5 percent (post- consumer + 1/2 post-industrial)
MRc4.2	Recycled Content, 10 percent (post- consumer + 1/2 post-industrial)
MRc5.1	Regional Materials, 20 percent Manufactured Regionally
MRc5.2	Regional Materials, 50 percent Extracted Regionally
MRc6	Rapidly Renewable Materials, 5 percent
MRc7	Certified Wood
EQc3.1	Construction IAQ Management Plan, During Construction
EQc3.2	Construction IAQ Management Plan, Before Occupancy
EQc4.1	Low-Emitting Materials, Adhesives and Sealants
EQc4.2	Low-Emitting Materials, Paints
EQc4.3	Low-Emitting Materials, Carpet
EQc4.4	Low-Emitting Materials, Composite Wood
IDc1	Innovation in Design

As with all architectural projects, clear construction documentation, including the written specifications, is important. This is perhaps even more so with LEED requirements because they are still relatively unfamiliar to contractors and, particularly, subcontractors. Current versions of MasterSpec (www.arcomnet.com/visitor/ masterspec/ms.html) have been modified to incorporate much of the necessary language for LEED projects into the standard specification sections.

The final certification application cannot be submitted to USGBC until construction is complete. Because this might be years after the design documentation is issued, USGBC has recently modified their process to permit a design-phase review. Projects may elect to submit "those credits that USGBC can reasonably adjudicate based on design-phase documentation" for an early review. While this review is not binding, USGBC will indicate the likelihood of credit achievement for these credits. This review provides useful feedback as the project moves into construction. Once a project team knows how many credits they are confident of getting, it can be easier to manage the subsequent changes during construction that might effect the final point count.

SUSTAINABLE DESIGN II

LEED-NC Case Study

Project:	Artists for Humanity EpiCenter, Boston, Massachusetts
Description:	23,500 sq. feet (2,180 sq. m) new headquarters for a nonprofit arts organization includes art studios, teaching spaces, and 5,000 ft² (465 m²) of gallery space. AFH demonstrates that it is possible to achieve the highest levels of sustainability on a very tight budget. The EpiCenter uses energy and water efficiently, incorporates recycled materials, makes full use of natural daylight, and promotes the health of its occupants.
Certification:	LEED-NC v2.0 Platinum (53 points)

Sustainable Sites: The urban site provided credits for density, brownfield and public transportation access. The site had been previously developed and was 100 percent impervious prior to the project's construction. The site plan provides a small, but effective open space and sunken garden.

Water Efficiency: Water for irrigation of the landscaped courtyard is provided by rainwater harvested from the roof and stored in a 1,500 gallon (5700 l.) storage tank. Along with low flow faucets, this strategy contributes to a total potable water use of 73,000 gal/yr (276,000 liters/yr) or 3.1 gal/sq ft (127 liters/sq meter)

Energy Efficiency: The project features three major energy conservation measures: natural ventilation, daylighting and a photovoltaic array. The energy efficient envelope and low energy lighting design provides a low cooling load that can be handled entirely without mechanical cooling in the Boston climate. The roof slope and massing was designed to provide a more ideal angle for the 42 kW PV array that provides 150 percent of the electricity for the building. The project is extremely energy efficient and earned all 10 LEED Energy credits plus an innovation credit for exemplary performance.

Materials: The artistic spirit of the facility is exhibited by an extensive use of creatively recycled materials including windshields from junked cars as balcony guardrails, and recycled fiberglass toilet partitions. Streetcar rails salvaged during utility work for the project were used as exterior railings.

Lessons Learned: According to the architects, "the most significant lesson learned is that green

FIGURE 25A

LEED has been used in a wide variety of project types. *Source: USGBC.*

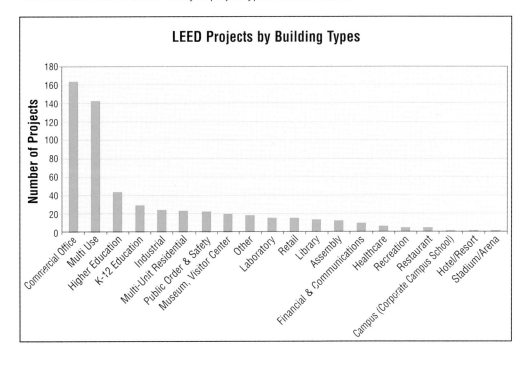

FIGURE 25B

The EpiCenter in Boston is an example of an urban infill project that incorporates green building design without compromising design or aesthetics. The 23,500 square foot [2200-m^2] building achieved a LEED-NC Platinum rating. Note the use of salvaged windshield glass for the guardrail around this interior space. *Photo by Richard Mandelkorn, courtesy of Arrowstreet.*

design does not have to be expensive. Although the EpiCenter received funding assistance for the photovoltaic array and other energy features, many of the sustainable features cost little or no more than standard materials and methods. Some actually cost less. Most will pay for any cost differential in savings on utilities or in comfort, health, and productivity of the occupants."

Cost: Project construction costs were $208 per square foot ($19/m^2) including the photovoltaic array.

Project Team:

Architect: Arrowstreet, Inc.
MEP Engineers: Zade Company, Inc.
Structural engineer: Rene Mugnier Associates, Inc.
Lighting Designer: US Lighting Consultants
Civil engineer: Samiotes Consultants, Inc.
Environmental building consultant: Building Science Engineering
Commissioning Agent: Shooshanian Engineering, Inc.
General Contractor: T.R. White Company, Inc.

FIGURE 25C

LEED-NC scorecard for the EpiCenter. *Source: USGBC.*

Artists For Humanity EpiCenter
LEED® Project # 1472
LEED Version 2 Certification Level: PLATINUM
13 October 2005

53 Points Achieved — Possible Points: 69

Certified 26 to 32 points   Silver 33 to 38 points   Gold 39 to 51 points   Platinum 52 or more points

10 Sustainable Sites — Possible Points: 14

Y	Prereq 1	Erosion & Sedimentation Control	
1	Credit 1	Site Selection	1
1	Credit 2	Urban Redevelopment	1
1	Credit 3	Brownfield Redevelopment	1
1	Credit 4.1	Alternative Transportation, Public Transportation Access	1
1	Credit 4.2	Alternative Transportation, Bicycle Storage & Changing Rooms	1
	Credit 4.3	Alternative Transportation, Alternative Fuel Refueling Stations	1
1	Credit 4.4	Alternative Transportation, Parking Capacity	1
	Credit 5.1	Reduced Site Disturbance, Protect or Restore Open Space	1
	Credit 5.2	Reduced Site Disturbance, Development Footprint	1
1	Credit 6.1	Stormwater Management, Rate and Quantity	1
1	Credit 6.2	Stormwater Management, Treatment	1
1	Credit 7.1	Landscape & Exterior Design to Reduce Heat Islands, Non-Roof	1
1	Credit 7.2	Landscape & Exterior Design to Reduce Heat Islands, Roof	1
1	Credit 8	Light Pollution Reduction	1

4 Water Efficiency — Possible Points: 5

1	Credit 1.1	Water Efficient Landscaping, Reduce by 50%	1
1	Credit 1.2	Water Efficient Landscaping, No Potable Use or No Irrigation	1
	Credit 2	Innovative Wastewater Technologies	1
1	Credit 3.1	Water Use Reduction, 20% Reduction	1
1	Credit 3.2	Water Use Reduction, 30% Reduction	1

17 Energy & Atmosphere — Possible Points: 17

Y	Prereq 1	Fundamental Building Systems Commissioning	
Y	Prereq 2	Minimum Energy Performance	
Y	Prereq 3	CFC Reduction in HVAC&R Equipment	
2	Credit 1.1	Optimize Energy Performance, 20% New/10% Existing	2
2	Credit 1.2	Optimize Energy Performance, 30% New/20% Existing	2
2	Credit 1.3	Optimize Energy Performance, 40% New/30% Existing	2
2	Credit 1.4	Optimize Energy Performance, 50% New/40% Existing	2
2	Credit 1.5	Optimize Energy Performance, 60% New/50% Existing	2
1	Credit 2.1	Renewable Energy, 5%	1
1	Credit 2.2	Renewable Energy, 10%	1
1	Credit 2.3	Renewable Energy, 20%	1
1	Credit 3	Additional Commissioning	1
1	Credit 4	Ozone Depletion	1
1	Credit 5	Measurement & Verification	1
1	Credit 6	Green Power	1

5 Materials & Resources — Possible Points: 13

Y	Prereq 1	Storage & Collection of Recyclables	
	Credit 1.1	Building Reuse, Maintain 75% of Existing Shell	1
	Credit 1.2	Building Reuse, Maintain 100% of Existing Shell	1
	Credit 1.3	Building Reuse, Maintain 100% Shell & 50% Non-Shell	1
1	Credit 2.1	Construction Waste Management, Divert 50%	1
1	Credit 2.2	Construction Waste Management, Divert 75%	1
	Credit 3.1	Resource Reuse, Specify 5%	1
	Credit 3.2	Resource Reuse, Specify 10%	1
1	Credit 4.1	Recycled Content	1
1	Credit 4.2	Recycled Content	1
	Credit 5.1	Local/Regional Materials, 20% Manufactured Locally	1
	Credit 5.2	Local/Regional Materials, of 20% Above, 50% Harvested Locally	1
	Credit 6	Rapidly Renewable Materials	1
1	Credit 7	Certified Wood	1

12 Indoor Environmental Quality — Possible Points: 15

Y	Prereq 1	Minimum IAQ Performance	
Y	Prereq 2	Environmental Tobacco Smoke (ETS) Control	
	Credit 1	Carbon Dioxide (CO_2) Monitoring	1
	Credit 2	Increase Ventilation Effectiveness	1
1	Credit 3.1	Construction IAQ Management Plan, During Construction	1
1	Credit 3.2	Construction IAQ Management Plan, Before Occupancy	1
1	Credit 4.1	Low-Emitting Materials, Adhesives & Sealants	1
1	Credit 4.2	Low-Emitting Materials, Paints	1
1	Credit 4.3	Low-Emitting Materials, Carpet	1
1	Credit 4.4	Low-Emitting Materials, Composite Wood	1
1	Credit 5	Indoor Chemical & Pollutant Source Control	1
1	Credit 6.1	Controllability of Systems, Perimeter	1
1	Credit 6.2	Controllability of Systems, Non-Perimeter	1
1	Credit 7.1	Thermal Comfort, Comply with ASHRAE 55-1992	1
	Credit 7.2	Thermal Comfort, Permanent Monitoring System	1
1	Credit 8.1	Daylight & Views, Daylight 75% of Spaces	1
1	Credit 8.2	Daylight & Views, Views for 90% of Spaces	1

5 Innovation & Design Process — Possible Points: 5

1	Credit 1.1	Innovation in Design, Exemplary Performance, EAc1	1
1	Credit 1.2	Innovation in Design, Innovative Elevator	1
1	Credit 1.3	Innovation in Design, Green Building Education	1
1	Credit 1.4	Innovation in Design, Exemplary Performance, EAc2	1
1	Credit 2	LEED® Accredited Professional	1

LEED FOR COMMERCIAL INTERIORS

In contrast to LEED-NC, which is difficult to apply to projects that are not new buildings or complete renovations, LEED-CI was developed specifically for interior fit-out projects that don't involve exterior renovations or extensive system upgrades. LEED-CI is ideally suited for tenant improvement projects in leased spaces. The applicable space types listed in the LEED-CI Reference Guide are "office, retail, restaurant, healthcare, hotel/resort, and education," but projects that have already been LEED-CI certified include spas, community centers, showrooms, food stores, and laboratories. (All registered and certified projects are listed on the USGBC web site.)

LEED-CI uses the same six categories as LEED-NC, but with different proportioning of points to reflect the typical scope of a tenant project. For example, the Sustainable Sites category has a much smaller share of credits in LEED-CI than in LEED-NC because there is typically little site work involved in these projects. On the other hand, Indoor Environmental Quality has a higher percentage of credits in LEED-CI reflecting the greater impact of tenant fit-out projects on the indoor environment and the health and well-being of the occupants.

Other important differences between NC and CI are related to the expected scope of work in tenant improvements. For example, including furniture and furnishings (FF&E) in LEED-NC the Materials and Resources category is optional, but not required. In LEED-CI, however, where FF&E is often a major portion of the project scope, there are credits relating specifically to furniture, and FF&E costs must be included in the materials credits. Another important difference is found in the Energy & Atmosphere category. The energy credits in LEED-NC are based on total energy use with lighting, heating, cooling, and similar loads all combined. Tenant fit-outs often have little control over the "base-building" HVAC system but usually do involve lighting design and selection of electrical devices and office equipment. LEED-CI recognizes this by separating the Optimize Energy Performance credits into individual subcategories related to lighting, HVAC, and equipment. This permits projects to be rewarded for those energy-efficiency strate-

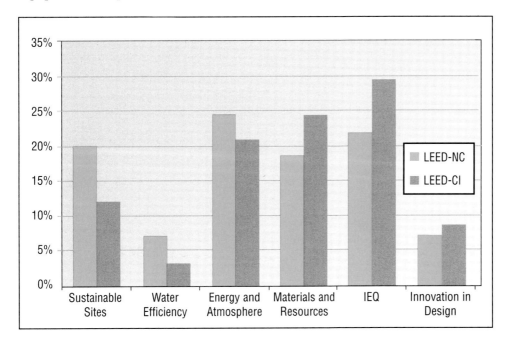

FIGURE 26

Comparison of the distribution of credits in each category for LEED for New Construction and LEED for Commercial Interiors. The variations reflect the differences in the design and construction scope between a new construction or full renovation project and a typical interiors project. *Source: USGBC.*

gies that are within their design scope without being significantly penalized by those that are outside their control.

Like LEED-NC, LEED-CI can be used as a tool to guide design decisions and material selections, but it can also be used in predesign phases of the project, particularly site selection.. The Sustainable Sites credits in LEED-CI are almost completely related to characteristics and environmental performance of the base building. Points are awarded if the project is located in a LEED-certified building, or a building with other positive green features, including:

- Location on a brownfield site
- Best-practice stormwater management
- Underground parking to help mitigate heat islands
- Green roof
- Water-efficient irrigation
- On-site renewable energy for five percent of the total building
- Location near public transit

The Sustainable Site requirements in LEED-CI can be an excellent "shopping list" for tenants looking for buildings in which to lease space. By including these criteria in the search, a tenant can ensure that they consider environmental values in their choice of location.

Also unique to LEED-CI are the credits related to the tenant lease. There are credits that discourage dedicated tenant parking, encourage separate electric submeters, and encourage direct billing of energy costs. LEED-CI can be used as a tool during negotiation of the lease. In fact, the LEED-CI Reference Guide provides a chart for each credit category showing its appropriate scheduling and decision point in the project timeline.

The certification process is similar to that of LEED-NC although there is no design phase review provided in LEED-CI.

FIGURE 27

Appropriate scheduling and decision points in the timeline for LEED-CI projects. *Source: USGBC, LEED for Commercial Interiors Reference Guide.*

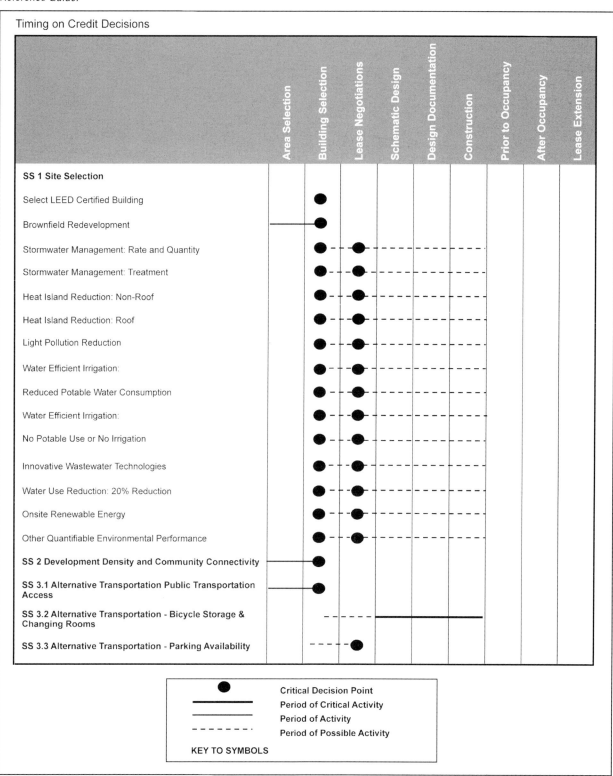

LEED-CI CASE STUDY

Project: Wallace Roberts & Todd, LLC (WRT) Main Office
Description: 28,000 square feet [2600 m^2] of offices for a planning, architecture, and landscape architecture practice. The space is the entire floor of a 32-story highrise in downtown Philadelphia, built in 1960s.
Certification: LEED-CI Gold (32 points)

FIGURE 28A

A tenant fit-out of 28,000 square feet [2,600 m^2] of office space, by Wallace, Roberts & Todd, LLC (WRT) and Partridge Architects. By focusing on a small number of effective strategies, including daylighting, indoor air quality, and material specifications, the project achieved a LEED for Commercial Interiors Gold rating with a relatively small added cost. *Photo by Dean Gazzo, Raber Photography.*

Sustainable Sites: One of the key criteria used in selecting a building was proximity to mass transit. This was decided after a survey revealed that 90 percent of WRT staffers commuted by public transportation, by bicycle, or on foot. LEED favors dense, urban sites because of their existing infrastructure, walkability, and minimizing disturbance of natural habitat and greenfield sites, so the choice of the center city Philadelphia building helped the project earn 4 of 7 Sustainable Sites points.

FIGURE 28B

Floor plan of the LEED-CI Gold-certified WRT office space showing a concentration of enclosed spaces near the building core to enhance daylighting access and views to the majority of occupied spaces. *Drawing by Wallace Roberts & Todd, LLC.*

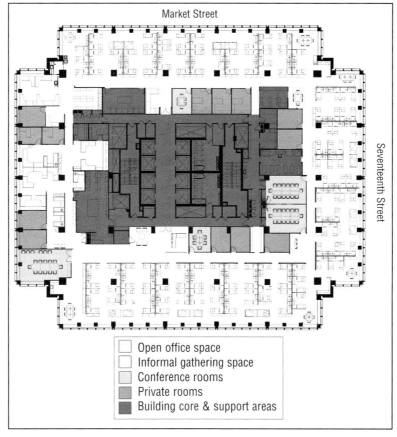

Market Street

Seventeenth Street

☐ Open office space
☐ Informal gathering space
▫ Conference rooms
▪ Private rooms
■ Building core & support areas

Design for Daylighting: There was a strong project goal to provide maximum access to views and daylight for all employees. This was incorporated from the beginning and led to a workspace layout that concentrated most of the enclosed spaces in the interior core, leaving the majority of the perimeter windows open to the unenclosed desks and work areas. Reflective film that had been installed on

FIGURE 28C

In the WRT office space, interior light shelves are part of the daylighting strategy. *Photo by Dean Gazzo, Raber Photography.*

the windows in the 1970s was replaced with a newer, high-performance coating that blocks as much of the solar heat gain as the old film but transmits twice the visible daylight. To ensure that energy savings were captured, the lighting designer modeled the space using daylight simulation software. Photosensors mounted on the windows measure the amount of natural light and control the level of electric illumination by switching on or off individual lamps within the luminaires.

Materials After lighting, the next largest part of this interior design project was furniture. The furniture manufacturer, Knoll, was selected partly for the high level of recycled content in their products and the proximity of one of their factories where many of the products would be made. Knoll's knowledge of LEED and their ability to provide the necessary LEED documentation was also a factor. This, along with a substantial quantity of reused furniture, helped the project to earn 7 out of 14 points in the Materials & Resources (M&R) category plus 2 more Innovation in Design points for "exemplary performance" on M&R credits.

Indoor Environmental Quality: Because many finishes used in interior construction emit toxic chemicals and VOCs, there was careful attention to the selection of paint, adhesives, carpet, and furniture that met the emissions requirements of the Indoor Environmental Quality (IEQ) category. Achieving IEQ credit 4.4 required avoiding the use of any particleboard containing formaldehyde. Wheatboard, a product made from agricultural waste without formaldehyde resins, was substituted for particleboard in all desktops and casework.

Lessons Learned: The interior construction industry is different from the new-construction industry in that the drawings and specifications are somewhat less detailed and construction times are shorter. The submittal process is often eliminated, particularly for typical products such as paints and glues. LEED certification, however, requires greater scrutiny of these products. It is important to communicate the importance of these key LEED product specifications and of the need for submittal review and approval.

Performance: While an installed energy submeter is not yet in use to provide consumption data, a postoccupancy evaluation was conducted for the project by the Center for the Built Environment at the University of California at Berkeley. The results indicated high levels of satisfaction with the daylighting, views, and indoor air quality, but less satisfaction with thermal and acoustic comfort. WRT has reported success in staff recruiting due to the LEED certification and the abundant views and natural light in the space.

Cost: Costs to the project related to green factors and meeting LEED criteria are estimated to be approximately $42,300 or three percent of the total cost:

Commissioning	$11,000
Miscellaneous construction adds	24,300
LEED documentation costs	5,000
USGBC Pilot Project fee	2,000
TOTAL	$42,300

Project Team:
Design Architect: Wallace Roberts & Todd
Executive Architect: Partridge Architects
MEP Engineers: Bruce Brooks & Associates
Lighting Designer: Dave Nelson & Associates
Commissioning Agent: Concord Facility Services
General Contractor: W.S. Cumby

FIGURE 29

LEED for Commercial Interiors scorecard for the WRT Headquarters project. *Source: Wallace Roberts & Todd, LLC.*

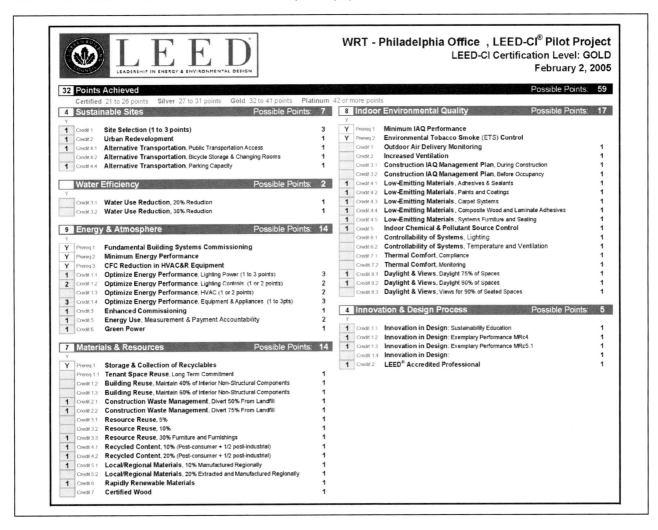

LEED FOR CORE AND SHELL

LEED for Core and Shell (LEED-CS) was developed for owners and developers who are constructing buildings intended for lease to or use by multiple, separate tenants. LEED-CS was conceived as a partner to the LEED-CI Rating System and is intended for projects that involve site, core, and shell infrastructure but not the individual tenant fit-out. LEED-CS focuses solely on the limited scope of construction over which the base building design and construction team has control. Nearly all of the LEED-CS-registered and -certified projects have been speculative office buildings, although the program is being used on a variety of other projects including retail shopping centers, healthcare facilities, government buildings, and mixed-use projects including residential.

LEED-CS uses the same six categories as LEED-NC and CI, but the distribution of points is shifted to recognize the unique aspects of core and shell development. Figure 30 compares the percentage of credit points in LEED-CS with those in LEED-CI. There is a significantly larger share of credits in the Sustainable Sites in the Core & Shell Rating System. This is appropriate because the owner/developer selects the site for the development and constructs the site infrastructure including parking, stormwater, planting, and so on. LEED-CS encourages developers to avoid greenfields and other inappropriate sites and to use ecologically sensitive strategies for landscaping, stormwater management, and site lighting. On the other hand, there is a smaller percentage of points available in the Materials & Resources and

FIGURE 30

Comparison of the distribution of credits in each category for LEED for Commercial Interiors and LEED for Core and Shell. The two systems are intended to be complementary. *Source: USGBC.*

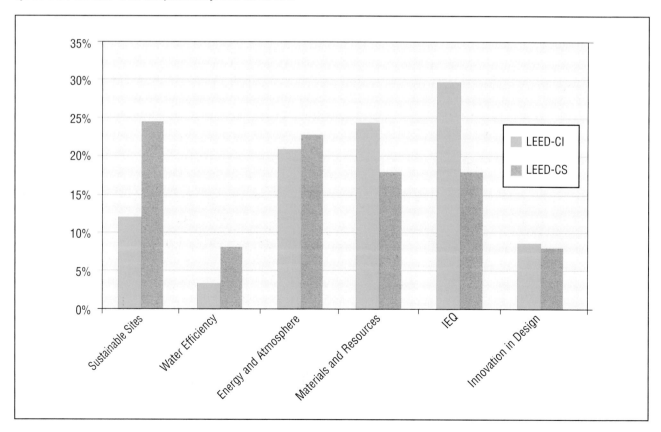

Indoor Environmental Quality categories, because these interior aspects are not usually a large part of the core-and-shell construction.

A unique aspect of LEED for Core & Shell is the ability to qualify for a "pre-certification." Precertification can be earned before construction based on the proposed design and a commitment by the team to "complete the building with these features and this level of performance." This allows the developer to market the building as a LEED project, thus distinguishing it in the marketplace. The precertification may also be used to qualify for certain incentive programs such as tax credits. Another unique category in LEED-CS is for Tenant Design and Construction Guidelines. A credit is awarded if the developer provides tenants with a tenant manual that "both educates and helps them implement sustainable design and constructions features in their tenant improvement build-out." This credit serves as both an educational tool and a bridge to LEED-CI for tenants who wish to construct a sustainable interior design for their space.

LEED-CS is a relatively new rating system, having been approved by the USGBC in July, 2006. Its growing use by large national real estate developers, as well as small local firms, is serving to educate this market sector about sustainable design. Although somewhat limited in its reach into the whole building by its focus on the core and shell, it does encourage the project team to consider site development and water and energy efficiency in ways that are not typical for speculative developments. For example, in Portland, OR, Gerding/Edlen Development Company, LLC renovated the Brewery Blocks into 1.7 million square feet [158,000 m²] of mixed-use space and certified the project in the LEED-CS pilot program. The building includes a vegetated roof, on-site 21.6-kilowatt solar photovoltaic array, and base building energy-conservation measures such as daylighting controls, interior light shelves, and high-efficiency HVAC systems, all with a total increase in construction costs of less than one percent. The performance benefits are estimated to include 20 percent less energy consumption, 25 percent less water use, and, perhaps most important for the developer, 85 percent of the space leased in one year at above-market rents.

FIGURE 31

Brewery Blocks is a 1.7 million-square-foot [158,000-m2] redevelopment in Portland, Oregon by Gerding/Edlen Development Company. *Photo: Gerding/Edlen Co.*

SUSTAINABLE DESIGN II

LEED-CI CASE STUDY

Project: One Crescent Drive, Philadelphia, Pennsylvania

Description: 110,000-square-foot [10,200 -m^2], four-story new office building on a brownfield site at the Philadelphia Naval Yard, a decommissioned Navy Base. Liberty Property Trust, the developer, is a publicly traded, $6.5 billion real estate investment trust which owns over 63 million square feet [5.85 million m^2] of office and industrial space throughout the United States and the United Kingdom.

LEED Certification: LEED-CS Platinum (pre-certified Gold)

Key Features: Much of the green performance for the project comes from intelligent application of off-the-shelf systems and technologies.

Sustainable Sites: The sitework included native landscaping and vegetated swales for stormwater management, allocation of preferred parking spaces for hybrid vehicles, and the use of an innovative reflective aggregate asphalt paving to reduce the heat island effect associated with blacktop.

    Water Efficiency: Although waterless urinals were not permitted by local code, the project did project a 30-percent water savings using automatic shut-off faucets, flow restricting aerators, and similar water-efficient fixtures.

    Energy & Atmosphere: Using off-the-shelf, high-efficiency equipment, heat recovery ventilation, and such simple architectural measures as sun shading and a reflective roof, the building is expected to use half the energy of a standard office building.

    Materials & Resources A wide variety of strategies were used related to materials and waste, including an aggressive recycling program that prevented 95 percent of construction debris from going to the landfill. Recycled waste slag was used as a substitute for 40 percent of the cement in the concrete mix, substantially lowering the embodied greenhouse gas (GHG) emissions. Forty percent of

FIGURE 32

One Crescent Drive is a speculative 110,000-square-foot [10,200-m2] office building on a brownfield site at a decommissioned Navy Base in Philadelphia developed by Liberty Property Trust. *Source: Re:Vision Architects.*

the materials were manufactured regionally and 30 percent were from recycled feedstock.

Indoor Environmental Quality: Although there are fewer credit opportunities in this category for LEED-CS projects, this project specified low-VOC finish materials and achieved an Innovation Credit for implementing a green-cleaning program that uses healthier, less toxic chemicals.

Project Team:

Developer, Owner, Manager: Liberty Property Trust
Design Architect: Robert A.M. Stern Architects
Architect of Record: Vitetta
Green Design Consultant: Re:Vision Architecture
Civil Engineer: Pennoni Associates
Landscape Architect: Synterra Ltd.
Contractor: L.F. Driscoll, Inc./ McKissack & McKissack

FIGURE 33

LEED Core and Shell scorecard for One Crescent Drive. *Source: Re:Vision Architects.*

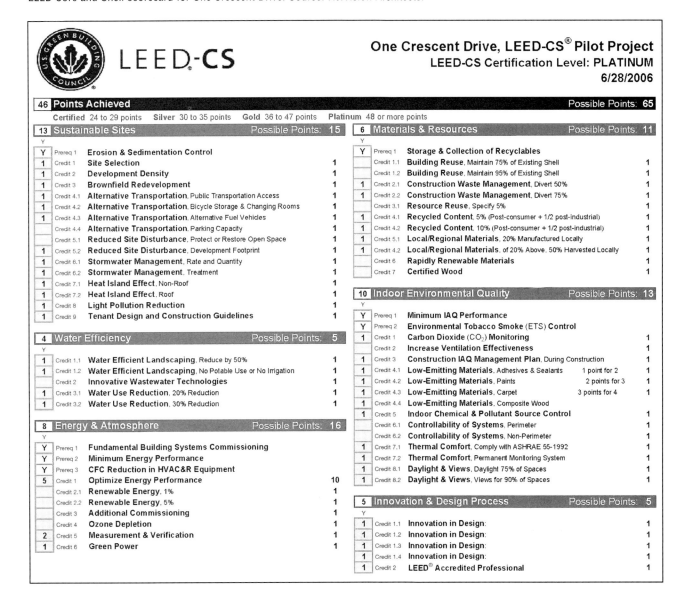

One Crescent Drive, LEED-CS® Pilot Project
LEED-CS Certification Level: PLATINUM
6/28/2006

46 Points Achieved — Possible Points: 65

Certified 24 to 29 points   Silver 30 to 35 points   Gold 36 to 47 points   Platinum 48 or more points

13 Sustainable Sites — Possible Points: 15

Y	Prereq 1	Erosion & Sedimentation Control	
1	Credit 1	Site Selection	1
1	Credit 2	Development Density	1
1	Credit 3	Brownfield Redevelopment	1
1	Credit 4.1	Alternative Transportation, Public Transportation Access	1
1	Credit 4.2	Alternative Transportation, Bicycle Storage & Changing Rooms	1
1	Credit 4.3	Alternative Transportation, Alternative Fuel Vehicles	1
	Credit 4.4	Alternative Transportation, Parking Capacity	1
	Credit 5.1	Reduced Site Disturbance, Protect or Restore Open Space	1
1	Credit 5.2	Reduced Site Disturbance, Development Footprint	1
1	Credit 6.1	Stormwater Management, Rate and Quantity	1
1	Credit 6.2	Stormwater Management, Treatment	1
1	Credit 7.1	Heat Island Effect, Non-Roof	1
1	Credit 7.2	Heat Island Effect, Roof	1
1	Credit 8	Light Pollution Reduction	1
1	Credit 9	Tenant Design and Construction Guidelines	1

4 Water Efficiency — Possible Points: 5

Y			
1	Credit 1.1	Water Efficient Landscaping, Reduce by 50%	1
1	Credit 1.2	Water Efficient Landscaping, No Potable Use or No Irrigation	1
	Credit 2	Innovative Wastewater Technologies	1
1	Credit 3.1	Water Use Reduction, 20% Reduction	1
1	Credit 3.2	Water Use Reduction, 30% Reduction	1

8 Energy & Atmosphere — Possible Points: 16

Y	Prereq 1	Fundamental Building Systems Commissioning	
Y	Prereq 2	Minimum Energy Performance	
Y	Prereq 3	CFC Reduction in HVAC&R Equipment	
5	Credit 1	Optimize Energy Performance	10
	Credit 2.1	Renewable Energy, 1%	1
	Credit 2.2	Renewable Energy, 5%	1
	Credit 3	Additional Commissioning	1
	Credit 4	Ozone Depletion	1
2	Credit 5	Measurement & Verification	1
1	Credit 6	Green Power	1

6 Materials & Resources — Possible Points: 11

Y	Prereq 1	Storage & Collection of Recyclables	
	Credit 1.1	Building Reuse, Maintain 75% of Existing Shell	1
	Credit 1.2	Building Reuse, Maintain 95% of Existing Shell	1
1	Credit 2.1	Construction Waste Management, Divert 50%	1
1	Credit 2.2	Construction Waste Management, Divert 75%	1
	Credit 3.1	Resource Reuse, Specify 5%	1
1	Credit 4.1	Recycled Content, 5% (Post-consumer + 1/2 post-industrial)	1
1	Credit 4.2	Recycled Content, 10% (Post-consumer + 1/2 post-industrial)	1
1	Credit 5.1	Local/Regional Materials, 20% Manufactured Locally	1
1	Credit 5.2	Local/Regional Materials, of 20% Above, 50% Harvested Locally	1
	Credit 6	Rapidly Renewable Materials	1
	Credit 7	Certified Wood	1

10 Indoor Environmental Quality — Possible Points: 13

Y	Prereq 1	Minimum IAQ Performance		
Y	Prereq 2	Environmental Tobacco Smoke (ETS) Control		
1	Credit 1	Carbon Dioxide (CO_2) Monitoring		1
	Credit 2	Increase Ventilation Effectiveness		1
1	Credit 3	Construction IAQ Management Plan, During Construction		1
1	Credit 4.1	Low-Emitting Materials, Adhesives & Sealants	1 point for 2	1
1	Credit 4.2	Low-Emitting Materials, Paints	2 points for 3	1
1	Credit 4.3	Low-Emitting Materials, Carpet	3 points for 4	1
1	Credit 4.4	Low-Emitting Materials, Composite Wood		1
1	Credit 5	Indoor Chemical & Pollutant Source Control		1
	Credit 6.1	Controllability of Systems, Perimeter		1
	Credit 6.2	Controllability of Systems, Non-Perimeter		1
1	Credit 7.1	Thermal Comfort, Comply with ASHRAE 55-1992		1
1	Credit 7.2	Thermal Comfort, Permanent Monitoring System		1
1	Credit 8.1	Daylight & Views, Daylight 75% of Spaces		1
1	Credit 8.2	Daylight & Views, Views for 90% of Spaces		1

5 Innovation & Design Process — Possible Points: 5

Y			
1	Credit 1.1	Innovation in Design:	1
1	Credit 1.2	Innovation in Design:	1
1	Credit 1.3	Innovation in Design:	1
1	Credit 1.4	Innovation in Design:	1
1	Credit 2	LEED® Accredited Professional	1

LEED for Existing Buildings

The title, "LEED for Existing Buildings" (LEED-EB) is often misunderstood. Many people assume it is the LEED rating system to use for renovations, but this is not so. LEED-EB is intended for facility managers and property owners who want to assess how well their buildings are really performing, and it addresses on-going maintenance policies that may have negative health or environmental effects, like pest control, cleaning, and landscape management. This rating system might be more appropriately named "LEED for Operations & Maintenance." It is unique among the LEED rating systems for commercial buildings in that it involves actual performance data. Therefore, LEED-EB projects will eventually provide a valuable database on building operations. At some point in the future, USGBC may decide to require periodic recertification using LEED-EB of all LEED certified projects.

LEED-EB in its current form requires a comprehensive assessment of building operations and maintenance. This is a valuable exercise for any building owner, but it can be a time-consuming and expensive effort. Probably for this reason, it is mostly large companies with substantial facilities that are tackling LEED-EB. A revised version of LEED-EB is expected in 2007 that will modify some of the more onerous requirements.

LEED-EB has also been used for older, pre-LEED projects that were constructed using sustainable design principles and whose owners wish to achieve recognition for their building's green performance. The JohnsonDiversey's global headquarters, located in Sturtevant, WI, is one example of this type of EB project. Other owners have sought a methodology for comparing a building's performance against other buildings of a similar type or within that owner's real estate portfolio. This was the case with the California Environmental Protection Agency Headquarters Building in Sacramento. The builder, Thomas Properties Group, LLC, used LEED-EB to benchmark its environmental performance. The process led to approximately $500,000 in upgrades to this 25-story, 950,000-square-foot [88,250-m²] office building and the awarding of a LEED-EB Platinum certification. The improvements generated a savings of over $600,000 in the first year, more than paying for the cost of the changes.

LEED-EB uses the same six credit categories as LEED-NC, but adds several additional prerequisites and a number of new credits related to on-going maintenance and facility operations. While many of these added requirements and credits reflect the potential conditions found in older buildings, others introduce performance standards that are not yet included in other LEED systems.

FIGURE 34

The California EPA headquarters is a 25-story, 950,000-square-foot [88,000-m²] office building that was awarded a LEED-EB Platinum certification. *Photo by John Swain Photography.*

New prerequisites under LEED-EB include a requirement that the building be at least two years old, have a minimum water efficiency (20 percent better than code), and undergo a required waste audit, asbestos abatement, and PCB removal. New credits include Sustainable Sites credits for an ecologically sensitive landscape management plan; Energy & Atmosphere credits for a building systems maintenance plan including staff training and the tracking and reporting of GHG emissions; Materials & Resources credits for recycling by occupants and reduced mercury in light bulbs; and Indoor Environmental Quality credits for documenting productivity and health improvements and green cleaning.

As noted, LEED-EB relies extensively on actual, documented building performance. It uses the U.S. EPA's ENERGY STAR Energy Performance Rating as the benchmark for energy performance, for example. The Energy & Atmosphere prerequisite for minimum energy performance requires an ENERGY STAR score of at least 60. These ratings are based on reported data from similar building types. A rating of 60 means the actual energy use intensity, in Btu per square foot per year, is better than 60 percent of all buildings of the same type. To achieve additional points, the project must have an ENERGY STAR Rating over 60: 1 point for a score of 63, two points for a score of 67, and so on up to 10 points for a 99.

Because LEED-EB is typically not used during an architectural design project, architects are only occasionally the leaders of these certification efforts. Practices that include facility maintenance services would, however, be wise to develop a familiarity with LEED-EB. As institutions and other multiple-building owners become comfortable with LEED on new construction, they may want to apply LEED standards to their entire portfolio. LEED-EB offers a useful tool to help architectural firms continue a relationship with such clients.

In spite of the clumsy and overly complicated process required by the current version of LEED-EB, this rating system can be valuable for architects because it helps illuminate the connection between design and ongoing building operations and maintenance. All architects will benefit from understanding what their clients need to do to maintain their buildings in an environmentally friendly manner. Considering on-going operational practices during design can lead to better-performing green buildings.

SUSTAINABLE DESIGN II

LEED-EB CASE STUDY

Project: JohnsonDiversey, Sturtevant, Wisconsin

Description: JohnsonDiversey's global headquarters is a three-story mixed-use facility constructed in 1997. The building floor area is 277,440 square feet [26,000 m²], of which 70 percent is office space and 30 percent is research laboratories. The building was designed according green-building principles, including high energy efficiency, extensive use of natural lighting, and individual control of workspace environments. Because it was built with sustainability in mind, applying LEED-EB to the building was primarily a matter of fine-tuning the building's operations practices and improving the documentation of existing sustainable practices. Stu Carron, Director of Global Facilities and Real Estate, enlisted the support of senior management to proceed with the LEED-EB evaluation. Jeff Furness, a LEED-Accredited Professional, reviewed facility operations and practices for a preliminary LEED-EB scoring of the facility. Based on his review, Furness and Carron identified the most achievable and cost-effective opportunities for change and developed a list of recommendations for achieving LEED-EB prerequisites and credits.

LEED Certification: The JohnsonDiversey Global Headquarters was certified LEED-EB Gold in March, 2004.

Key Features:

◆ Energy savings exceeding $90,000 per year
◆ Use of collected stormwater for turfgrass irrigation reducing potable water use by 2-4 million gallons [7,500-15,000 cu. m.] per year
◆ Documented recycling of 50 percent of site-generated solid waste
◆ Policies for integrated pest management, cleaning-worker training, certified cleaning chemicals, systems approaches to cleaning, and cleaning equipment.
◆ CO_2 monitoring
◆ Individual/personal environment controls (for air flow, temperature, acoustics, and lighting) significantly increasing occupant comfort and virtually eliminating temperature-related complaints
◆ Increased occupant interest and involvement in environmental aspects of building operations

Sustainable Sites: The JohnsonDiversey project developed and instituted a low-impact site and building exterior chemical/fertilizer/pest management program in summer and low-impact snow removal and management program in winter. It established native prairie vegetation for extensive site areas, and the company hired a consultant to monitor and assess the health of the site.

FIGURE 35

The 277,000-square-foot [26,000-m2] headquarters for JohnsonDiversey was built in 1997 before LEED was publicly available. Certifying the facility under LEED for Existing Buildings was a way to recognize the green performance of the project. *Source: Stuart Carron.*

Water Efficiency: The project called for the installation and testing of a variety of low-flow fixtures and adopted successful measures such as replacement flush valves to achieve a level of water consumption 32 percent lower than code.

Energy & Atmosphere: Because the JohnsonDiversey facility has a large amount of laboratory space, it does not fit easily in any of the available ENERGY STAR building types. This made it a challenge to accurately model the baseline energy use for the building. JohnsonDiversey worked closely with the LEED-EB Pilot Program Committee to develop an appropriate procedure and then had consultants build and test the model to meet the Energy & Atmosphere prerequisite for minimum energy performance.

Materials & Resources. The required waste audit enabled JohnsonDiversey to document that over 50 percent of waste from the facility was already being recycled. In addition, the company instituted purchasing policies to encourage the use of recycled products, those made locally or regionally, and similarly alternative products.

Indoor Environmental Quality: JohnsonDiversey installed CO_2 sensors in the mixed-air plenums at all major air handlers to alert building operators when is the carbon dioxide level reached 530 parts per million (ppm) above ambient conditions. they developed and adopted a policy for low-environmental-impact cleaning fluids and housekeeping.

Project Team:

Developer, Owner, Manager: JohnsonDiversey
Project Manager: Stu Carron
Controls Subcontractor: Johnson Controls
LEED Accredited Professional: Jeff Furness

FIGURE 36

LEED for Existing Buildings scorecard for the JohnsonDiversey headquarters. *Source: USGBC.*

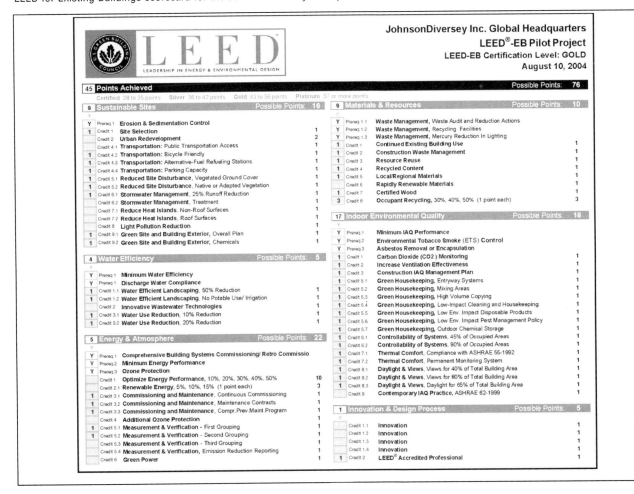

SUSTAINABLE DESIGN II

LEED for Homes

The vast majority of projects registered or certified under all of the LEED rating systems described to date have been commercial buildings. The home building industry is very different from the commercial building industry, and the attempts to use the initial versions of LEED on low-rise residential projects, particularly single family houses, was frustrating at best. Using the model of the many local and regional green home building programs found around the United States, LEED for Homes (LEED-H) was developed to help move the mainstream home building industry toward more sustainable practices (www.usgbc.org/DisplayPage.aspx?CMSPageID=147).

LEED–H originally focused on production builders of single-family houses to recognize the top 25 percent of performers in a variety of environmental categories. The pilot version of LEED-H was also applied to multifamily and affordable housing. Recognizing the different delivery methods for these types of projects, LEED-H has a certification process different from that of the other LEED rating systems. The key distinction is that certification is not managed centrally from the national USGBC office, but regionally using a network of LEED for Homes Providers. These providers have a central role in LEED-H. They are responsible for "recruiting builders, coordination of raters, certification of LEED Homes, quality assurance for the certifications, facilitation of trainings for all stakeholders in their local market, and coordination with USGBC and the local USGBC chapter." This decentralization is in keeping with the proliferation of local chapters of USGBC, as well as reflecting the regional diversity of the home building industry.

Another key difference in the process is that these providers will provide field verification of the installation of LEED-H-required features along with actual performance testing. This field verification, being tested as part of the pilot demonstration phase, is partly an adaptation of the commissioning prerequisite and credit from the more commercially focused LEED products, that requires actual field testing. This on-site inspection will provide an excellent confirmation of the quality and expected performance of the house but will also add to the overall cost of certification. Based on the experience of other green residential rating systems, including the ENERGY STAR program, combining the rigor of the requirements with the cost and "market friendliness" of LEED-H certification will be a delicate balancing act.

To better fit the homebuilding industry, LEED-H expands and rearranges the credit categories, adding two new ones: Location & Linkages (LL) and Homeowner Awareness (HA). The Location & Linkages category incorporates credits related to site selection, such as avoiding environmentally sensitive sites and choosing higher density or infill sites with close proximity to infrastructure and community resources. The Homeowner Awareness credit is for providing an "owner's manual" along with basic training regarding the green features of the house, the LEED rating, and how to operate the systems and maintain the house. The other six categories match those from the other LEED rating systems.

Certifying a residence using LEED-H involves satisfying both design and construction requirements and executing a sufficient number of the optional measures to meet the minimum point total. The sliding scale, from Certified to Platinum, is used the same here as with other LEED programs. A preliminary rating includes a design review as well as actual performance testing of a typical example of the house. The final rating for each house is provided after all inspections are successfully passed and the project documentation is completed. The provider issues the certification once the project documentation is reviewed and approved. For production builders certifying a number of similar houses, a sampling protocol is provided that only requires the actual testing and inspection of one out of every seven for each design model, except for Platinum ratings, which require individual verification.

The LEED for Homes rating system, in the pilot version current at the time of this writing, ensures that the house will include a number of environmentally friendly green features. Mandatory requirements for site treatment—such as leaving portions of larger sites undisturbed and limiting lawns to specific conditions—will help address some of the worst aspects of new housing developments. Requirements in the Indoor Environmental Quality category should help provide a healthy environment, or at least eliminate the contribution to unhealthy conditions that building materials and systems often make. Mandatory measures for the other categories should guarantee that LEED-H houses will do better than conventional ones at conserving water, materials, and energy.

The list of optional credits provides an excellent summary of many sustainable design opportunities in house design and construction and can help inform homebuilders about potential measures they can take to produce a green product. One of the more controversial credits rewards houses that are smaller than the national average and deducts points for houses that are larger than average. The rationale for this Materials & Resources credit is that smaller houses consume fewer resources than larger ones.

An innovative credit encourages the implementation of a "durability plan" that protects key building components and systems from degradation over time due to wind and moisture. Projects can achieve up to five points for this credit, depending on their climate, with houses in "wet regions" having the potential to earn more than those in "dry" areas.

It is worth noting that the ENERGY STAR for Homes program is closely tied to LEED-H. Homebuilders who are already building ENERGY STAR Homes have a distinct advantage in qualifying their projects for LEED-H. Meeting the ENERGY STAR requirements (with third-party testing) is a shortcut to achieving up to 16 Energy & Atmosphere points. Including the ENERGY STAR "indoor air package" provides a similar path to achieving 10 points in Indoor Environmental Quality.

LEED for Neighborhood Development

One of the most innovative developments in LEED is the LEED for Neighborhood Development (LEED-ND) (www.usgbc.org/DisplayPage.aspx?CMSPageID=148). This is a joint venture of USGBC, the Congress for New Urbanism (CNU), and the Natural Resources Defense Council (NRDC). It is intended to "integrate the principles of smart growth, urbanism, and green building into the first national standard for neighborhood design." Some calculations allocate half of all climate-change effects to our current land-use practices. It is certainly true that even highly energy-conserving buildings located away from other infrastructure and requiring extensive automobile travel are not energy efficient in the larger context. Responding to criticisms of LEED as too "building focused," LEED-ND reinforces the importance of location, proximity to public transit systems, pedestrian friendliness, and community connectivity in reducing the overall environmental impact of development and construction.

The LEED-ND rating system is still in development at this writing. An early draft rearranges the credit categories significantly in comparison to the other LEED rating systems. It uses four major categories called Location Efficiency; Environmental Preservation; Compact, Complete & Connected Neighborhoods; and Resource Efficiency.

LEED Application Guides

Certain building types have unique requirements that affect their pattern of energy and water consumption, their indoor conditions, or other aspects of their environmental footprint. Early in LEED's history, it became apparent that it would be difficult to apply LEED standards to hospitals and laboratories, for example, due to their unique requirements for occupant safety and health, and their unavoidably high energy intensities. Other building types, such as schools and retail facilities, have special requirements as well. The quality of the indoor environment and its effect on children's health and learning is paramount in schools. Retail spaces have relatively few full time occupants, and their design is frequently a site adaptation of a standard design.

To accommodate these unique conditions, application guides are being developed for these four use types—health care, laboratories, schools, and retail. These application guides will serve as tools to adapt and interpret LEED-NC and the other versions for these particular building types.

FIGURE 37

LEED for Neighborhood Development will take LEED beyond buildings to recognize development projects that successfully protect and enhance the overall health, natural environment, and quality of life of communities. *Site plan courtesy Wallace Roberts & Todd, LLC.*

BECOMING A LEED ACCREDITED PROFESSIONAL

More than 28,000 professionals around the world have passed the LEED Accreditation Exam and are LEED Accredited Professionals (APs). This large number would seem to indicate the high value the design and construction professions place on this credential. Increasingly, requests for proposals (RFPs) for architectural design services require the participation of a LEED AP on the design team, particularly RFPs from government agencies. To date, every LEED certification has achieved the Innovation & Design Process Credit for having a LEED AP as a key member of the project team.

Is there value beyond the credential and the extra LEED point in becoming accredited? The LEED for New Construction v2.1 exam, introduced in 2004, was a much more rigorous test than the original v2.0 exam and thus served as a better indicator of knowledge of LEED and green building. In late 2006, the accreditation process shifted again when USGBC began offering three new exams. Individuals may now select an exam with their preferred emphasis from the three major versions of LEED—New Construction, Commercial Interiors, and Existing Buildings. Successful completion of any one of these tests leads to LEED Accreditation. USGBC does not intend to distinguish between those who passed the various tests. The market, however, may value the distinction, and many LEED APs will undoubtedly indicate which version they passed on their business cards, brochures, and proposals, if it seems advantageous.

As with the Architect Registration Exam*, there are many approaches to preparing for the LEED Exam. The USGBC offers educational workshops on the various LEED versions around the country. While not specifically advertised

---

LEED ACCREDITATION EXAMS

Existing Buildings: The LEED-EB Exam verifies that an individual possesses the knowledge and skills necessary to support and encourage the operation, upgrade, and project team integration required for implementation of LEED on existing building projects. The exam tests an individual's understanding of the practices and principles of green building operations and upgrades and familiarity with LEED-EB requirements, resources, and processes.

Commercial Interiors: The LEED-CI Exam verifies that an individual understands green commercial interior design practices and principles, and is familiar with LEED-CI requirements, resources, and processes. LEED Accredited Professionals who pass the LEED-CI Exam track will help meet the growing demand from the private and public sectors for green commercial interiors.

New Construction and Major Renovations: The LEED-NC exam verifies that an individual possesses the knowledge and skills necessary to participate in the design process to support and encourage the design integration required by LEED and to streamline the application and certification process.

Source: USGBC web site www.usgbc.org

as exam prep workshops, they do offer a comprehensive view of the LEED Rating System and processes—two key aspects of the exam. USGBC also offers an online study course. Some local chapters have developed study guides and flash cards for preparation. Other chapters and individual firms have organized study groups. The "textbook" for the exam is the *LEED Reference Guide* for the each version. The *Reference Guide* includes the entire LEED Rating System, as well the references, calculation methods, definitions, and other considerations necessary for understanding and documenting each LEED credit and point. The reference guides are organized by the credit category—Sustainable Sites, Water Efficiency, and so on. Many people have found it helpful to study these sections as a way to organize their preparation.

Because many LEED credits refer to standards published by other organizations, it is helpful to have a general knowledge of these documents and the issues they address with respect to LEED. These third-party standards include:

- ASHRAE Standard 90.1-2004* Energy Standard for Buildings Except Low-Rise Residential Buildings
- ASHRAE Standard 62.1-2004* Ventilation for Acceptable Indoor Air Quality
- ASHRAE Standard 55-2004* Thermal Comfort Conditions for Human Occupancy.
- Green Seal Standards for VOC emissions in paints and adhesives
- South Coast Air Quality Management District Rule 1113, VOC limits for Architectural Coatings and Rule 1168, VOC Limits for Adhesives
- U.S. EPA Compendium of Methods for the Determination of Air Pollutants in Indoor Air
- Sheet Metal and Air Conditioning Contractors' National Association (SMACNA) IAQ Guidelines for Occupied Buildings under Construction, 1995*

or appropriate version referenced by the LEED standard

LEED ACCREDITATION EXAM
Content Areas
SECTION 1:

Knowledge of LEED Credit Intents and Requirements (27 questions)

- Apply LEED definitions consistently across all credits
- Establish level of knowledge of LEED credit intents requirements, submittals, technologies, and strategies for site, water, energy, materials, and IEQ credit categories
- Describe format and process for achieving Innovation in Design credits

SECTION 2:

Coordinate Project and Team (17 questions)

- Gather all project information and requirements to support the LEED process
- Manage coordination of multiple disciplines to achieve LEED certification
- Identify standards that support LEED credits
- Identify opportunities for integrated design and credit synergies to support LEED certification
- Identify critical path elements and schedule to implement LEED process

SECTION 3: Implement LEED Process (15 questions)

- Select appropriate LEED rating system for project scope
- Register project for LEED certification on-line
- Demonstrate knowledge of Credit Interpretation Rulings process and resources
- Manage LEED documentation/certification process
- Manage and complete letter templates
- Draft and review innovation credits

SECTION 4:

Verify, Participate In, and Perform Technical Analyses Required for LEED Credits (14 questions)

- Verify compliance of technical work products created by other team members
- Participate in and guide the development of technical analyses with design professionals
- Perform technical analyses to verify compliance with LEED requirements

Source: USGBC LEED Professional Accreditation Candidate Handbook, November, 2005

The LEED exams are multiple choice, computer-based examinations offered in testing centers around the country. The *LEED Professional Accreditation Candidate Handbook* available on the USGBC web site provides contact information for scheduling the exam. There are 73 randomly selected questions. You are allowed up to one hour and 45 minutes to complete the exam, and you will be told your score immediately upon finishing. If you answer correctly to 39 or more (53 percent) of the questions, you pass.

CRITICISMS OF LEED

LEED has been successful at beginning to transform the market for green buildings, a stated goal of the USGBC. However, as a volunteer-driven effort that requires consensus based decision-making, LEED is not perfect and has its detractors. USGBC has responded to many of the criticisms by modifying LEED credits or processes. At the time of this writing, a major overhaul is underway that will lead to a new version, LEED, expected in 2008.

One frequent criticism has been that LEED adds too much to the cost of a project. The potential for added construction costs for LEED or green buildings is addressed in a later section. There are also costs for fees and services related to LEED documentation. These include the required commissioning and energy calculations, as well as the cost of managing the LEED process—keeping track of the LEED credits and documentation, submitting the package to USGBC, responding to questions during the process, and so on.

Commissioning is a service that will add cost to a project initially, but in most cases, it provides immediate benefits as an independent review of both construction documents as well as postconstruction system start-up. Commissioning also provides long-term savings in subsequent building operations. Many institutional and government owners are commissioning their buildings as a matter of policy, whether pursuing LEED or not, because they have seen the benefits in fewer HVAC and control system problems, fewer contractor call-backs, and more-efficiently running systems.

As for energy consulting, it is slowly becoming more common, but is still considered an additional service on most projects. In the experience of many project teams, the cost of a thorough energy study that helps optimize the design of the building and systems has a high value and short payback time. The cost of the energy consulting can often be saved after one year of operation due to improved energy efficiency. For small projects, LEED provides lower-cost alternatives to full commissioning and energy-study requirements.

While there is a value to the commissioning and energy analysis services that most owners recognize, the benefit of LEED certification is not always as clear. The cost of managing the LEED process along with the fees paid to the USGBC, does cause many owners to balk at pursuing LEED certification, particularly for smaller projects. In response to the cost of LEED documentation, USGBC streamlined the process in 2005 and introduced *LEED On Line*, a web-based method of registering, managing, and submitting LEED documentation. In addition, the fees paid to USGBC were reworked with a flat rate for initial registration ($450 for members, $600 for nonmembers), a sliding scale for certification, and reduced fees for projects under 50,000 square feet [4,645600 m²]. While the early responses have been positive, it is not yet clear as of this writing how much effect these measures have had on the cost or use of LEED certification.

Many architects and owners simply use LEED as a guideline only and avoid the costs of certification. They rely on the LEED checklist to educate teams on green building design and suggest strategies to pursue. There is nothing wrong with this approach, and it may inspire some projects to go farther than they might otherwise. However, the benefit of going through the full certification process is greatly improved assurance that the built project is in fact a green building and that any changes to the design made during construction have not compromised its environmental performance. The experience of many teams who have used LEED both formally and informally suggests that the final review of the certification process is critical to maintaining the integrity of the design, even for the most motivated architects and owners.

Another criticism of LEED is its inability to weight credits and categories for different climates where ecological conditions suggest different priorities. For example, water only accounts for seven percent of the credits in LEED-NC v2.0 whether the project is in Seattle or Phoenix. Regional variations have already been introduced in some credits, such as Stormwater Design in LEED-NC and Durability Plan in

FIGURE 38

LEED On Line is an Internet submittal tool intended to make the LEED certification process easier and more convenient. *Source: USGBC, www.usgbc.org/ DisplayPage.aspx? CMSPageID=277&.*

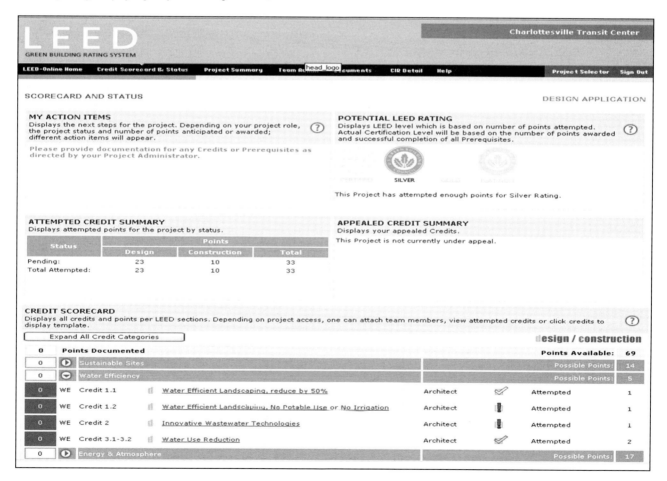

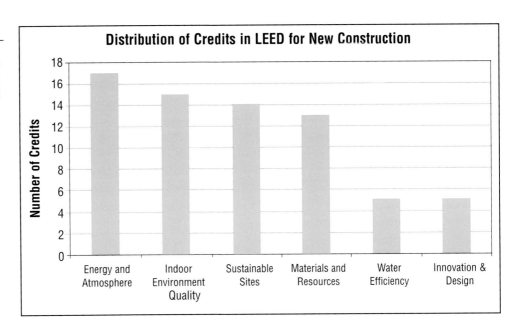

LEED-H. For version 3.0, LEED is expected to include some form of bioregional weightings into the rating system.

As LEED has been adopted as an incentive or requirement for particular project types, it is increasingly being used on projects where teams may not completely agree philosophically with the approach. In these cases, LEED may become more of a bureaucratic chore and less of a tool to help the project achieve the highest possible cost-effective environmental performance. This has led to criticism of LEED as encouraging "point chasing" at the expense of true environmental performance. Like any tool, how it is used can affect the outcome. The lack of consistent weighting of credits in LEED—however difficult or impossible that might be to achieve—can lead teams to seek the cheapest, easiest path to the desired LEED rating level.

This approach may not really be a problem as long as the prerequisites in LEED are maintained as adequate baselines exceeding code requirements, ensuring that even the lowest level of certification can be a "leader in environmental and energy design." There is a strong educational value of going through LEED and developing an understanding of how sustainable design can reduce the environmental impacts of buildings. If using LEED helps educate the mainstream building design industry, perhaps some point chasing is an acceptable trade-off.

One final negative occasionally voiced about LEED relates to its energy metrics. The LEED-NC, -CI, and –CS versions all use energy cost as the performance measurement because cost is an accessible metric that owners and architects can easily understand. With the growing emphasis on climate change, many people believe CO_2 emissions or GHG should be the assessment metric for energy use in LEED, as it is in BREEAM. USGBC's 2006 commitment to the Wingspread Principles (www.summits.ncat.org/energy_climate/statement.php) on global climate change, and to becoming a "carbon-neutral" organization reflects this growing sense of urgency about GHG. LEED v3.0 is expected to address this issue directly by shifting the energy measurements toward emissions and away from costs.

OTHER RATING SYSTEMS

LEED is not the only green building rating system in use in the United States, but it is the best known and most widely used. Partly in response to the perceived high cost and effort needed to achieve LEED standards, a simpler self-assessment tool known as Green Globes (www.thegbi.com/commercial/aboutgreenglobes/) was introduced in the United States in 2004 by the Green Building Initiative (GBI). GBI is based on a Canadian version that was, in turn, based originally on BREEAM.

Green Globes, version 1 shares many similarities with LEED. It has seven categories of environmental performance actions for which points are earned. There are four levels of Green Globes ratings based on the number of points received. Many of the individual items are similar or identical to credits in LEED. The key differences are that the rating is a self-assessment, it is generated at the completion of the construction documents phase, and the evaluation is conducted via an online questionnaire. To receive an official Green Globes rating, however, the project must pass an on-site inspection by a GBI-approved verifier.

There are a few interesting differences between LEED and Green Globes in their categories and recommended measures. For example, in the Project Management category the GBI system tries to encourage integrated design by giving points for "holding a collaboration session… to discuss sustainable design goals" and for identifying "measurable, environmental/sustainability performance goals" during the early stages of design. In the Water section, points are awarded for using less water in cooling towers, something that requires an Innovation in Design Credit in LEED-NC. In the Resources, Building Materials and Solid Waste section, Green Globes encourages teams to use available LCA tools by awarding points for using either BEES or the Athena Environmental Impact Estimator to select materials for those building systems that these LCA tools currently address. Again, in LEED, this would currently require an Innovation credit.

One standard in GBI that is significantly lower than its LEED counterpart relates to certified lumber. Whereas LEED recognizes only the FSC for wood certification, GBI awards points for any of several industry-sponsored wood certification systems, which it treats as equals to FSC. Some critics argue that LEED should give more credit than it currently does for wood as a renewable resource, but few objective observers would give equal standing to all of the certification programs that Green Globes does.

Green Globes Rating Scale:

85–100%		Reserved for select building designs which serve as national or world leaders in energy and environmental performance. The project introduces design practices that can be adopted and implemented by others.
70–84%		Demonstrates leadership in energy and environmental design practices and a commitment to continuous improvement and industry leadership.
55–69%		Demonstrates excellent progress in achieving eco-efficiency results through current best practices in energy and environmental design.
35–54%		Demonstrates movement beyond awareness and commitment to sound energy and environmental design practices by demonstrating good progress in reducing environmental impacts.

FIGURE 40

Although the Green Globes rating system has a few important differences, it is similar to LEED in many respects, such as its four tiers of certification. *Source: Green Globes, www.thegbi.com/commercial/aboutgreenglobes/.*

GBI has lobbied vigorously in the United States for being considered an "equal" to LEED and has had some legislative success in a few state mandate programs. As of mid-2006, Green Globes appears to be a somewhat simplified version of LEED with some interesting additional measures. GBI does not yet appear to have the infrastructure in place for third-party verification, and there are few rated projects listed on their web site.

GBI intends to make Green Globes an ANSI standard. ANSI standards can be easily written into codes and legislation, but the ANSI standards development process is designed to produce "minimum standards," or the least common denominator. Most other green building rating systems, like LEED, are designed to be "leadership" standards that push the envelope beyond minimum performance. As a response to the need for code-usable language, ASHRAE, along with USGBC and the American Institute of Architects (AIA), has initiated the development of a new standard, Standard 189.

According to ASHRAE, "Standard 189, Standard for the Design of High-Performance Green Buildings Except Low-Rise Residential Buildings will provide minimum requirements for the design of sustainable buildings to balance environmental responsibility, resource efficiency, occupant comfort and well-being, and community sensitivity." The intention is that Standard 189 will be an ANSI-accredited standard that could be incorporated into building codes. It is also expected that the standard will eventually become a prerequisite under LEED. If incorporated into building codes, the standard would potentially raise the level of environmental performance of all commercial buildings and have a major effect on the design and construction industry.

Local and State Ratings

A number of state and municipal governments have adopted LEED for use in their own self-funded projects (www.usgbc.org/ShowFile.aspx?DocumentID=691).

Often they simply set a minimum target (LEED Silver, for instance) but in some cases, they include other requirements to augment LEED. For example, Cook County, IL, requires LEED certification for all county-funded projects but also requires them to "earn a minimum of 8 credits in the Energy & Atmosphere category to ensure best life-cycle returns." In San Francisco, all municipal new construction and major renovations over 5,000 square feet [465 m²] must achieve LEED Silver certification, a LEED-accredited professional must be a member of each design team, and the LEED credit for additional commissioning must be earned for all projects.

FIGURE 41

The Florida Green Building Coalition has developed a regionally adapted rating system called the Green Commercial Building Designation. *Source: Florida Green Building Coalition, floridagreenbuilding.org/.*

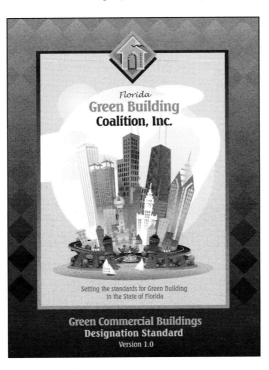

In some cases, states or cities have even developed their own commercial building rating systems to accommodate their unique conditions. Florida's Green Commercial Building Designation, developed by the Florida Green Building Coalition, is modeled on LEED but expands and modifies it to fit the specific environmental conditions in that state. For example, this standard offers a greater emphasis on water conservation by adding more credits in this category, and adds a new section called Disaster Mitigation related to hurricanes, floods, wildfires, and termites.

Other Residential Rating Systems

Prior to the initiation of LEED-H, a number of local homebuilders associations (HBAs) or local governments developed green homebuilding standards. The Austin (Texas) Green Building Program is one of the oldest and most respected local programs; it won an award for Local Government Initiatives at the United Nations Earth Summit in Rio de Janeiro in 1993. (www.austinenergy.com/ Energy%20Efficiency/Programs/ Green%20Building/index.htm) Atlanta's EarthCraft House program is another old and respected program originally started by the Southface Institute and the Greater Atlanta Area Homebuilders Association and since expanded to the entire Southeast region. (www.earthcrafthouse.com/) Colorado Built Green is one of the largest eco-friendly homebuilder programs with over 100 builders as members. (www.builtgreen.org/) These local and regional organizations can tailor their residential rating systems to meet the particular requirements of climate, culture, and economy.

To support those areas and local HBAs that have not yet instituted their own programs, the National Association of Home Builders (NAHB) developed the Model GREEN Home Building Guidelines. A point-based system with Bronze, Silver, and Gold levels, these are guidelines only and are not accompanied by a verification infrastructure. They can be used as a base on which local groups can create their own programs and provide suggestions for appropriate verification data. It should be noted that the NAHB guidelines omit most of the on-site, third-party inspections found in LEED-H, ENERGY STAR Homes, and many of the other existing programs.

International Rating Systems

Green building is recognized around the world as an important means to limit climate change and other environmental impacts. While LEED has been used or

FIGURE 42A, 42B, 42C

Several local and regional rating programs for green houses. *Logos from Colorado Built Green, Earth Craft House, and the Austin Energy Green Building Program.*

adapted for use in many countries, including Canada, China, Mexico, and India, other countries have developed their own systems with different conceptual approaches. BREEAM, described below, is commonly used in the United Kingdom.

Japan has developed the Comprehensive Assessment System for Building Environmental Efficiency (CASBEE) with a somewhat different approach to the final assessment. While the various categories of assessment are similar to those in LEED, CASBEE uses a different methodology to express the evaluation "score." The developers have identified a distinct difference between the building performance and environmental performance indicators. The "Building Environmental Quality & Performance" assessment chiefly measures interior environmental quality indicators such as air quality, acoustics, thermal comfort, and so on. These also include more qualitative performance assessments such as durability, flexibility, landscaping, and outdoor amenities. Within a separate category, CASBEE addresses "Reduction of Building Environmental Loading" factors that have effects outside of the property line. These include energy use, water consumption, air pollution, and local infrastructure. The final "Building Environmental Efficiency" score is a ratio of these two sets of metrics, providing a balance between the human and ecological impacts. In this system, a very "eco-efficient" building with low energy and water use, but with poor indoor air quality, acoustics, and durability, for example, might not score as well as one that had only an average score on energy conservation, for example but a high score on interior quality. This approach might have prevented the problems of early LEED buildings whose occupants reported poor acoustic quality.

FIGURE 43

Japan's CASBEE system considers two main types of environmental impact: within the building and outside. The BEE score combines both. *Source: CASBEE, http://www.ibec.or.jp/ CASBEE/english/overviewE.htm.*

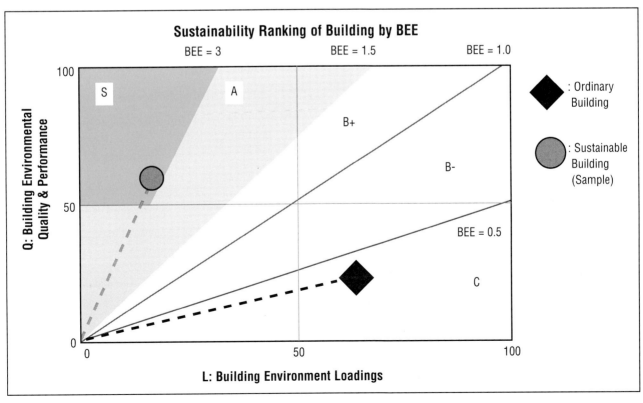

While more focused on academic and research uses, the Canadian "GB Tool" also represents a different approach from LEED. GB Tool includes a wider range of assessments with categories for "long-term performance" and "social & economic aspects." GB Tool, as appropriate for research, requires more precise predictions of performance and impact than LEED and thus can be normalized more effectively to compare buildings of similar type and climate. Perhaps the most important difference, however, is that GB Tool assesses buildings in all major categories, not just those categories that the owner/design team chooses. This identifies areas in which the building is a poor performer, as well as those in which it does well, providing a more complete picture of overall environmental performance.

ECONOMICS OF SUSTAINABLE BUILDINGS

DO GREEN BUILDINGS COST MORE?

Whether green buildings cost more is probably the most common question asked about sustainable design, with the follow-up often being: "how much more?" While the building industry generally understands that "you get what you pay for," there remains a fixation on the first costs for green buildings. The answer to the question, "do green buildings cost more?" is, of course, "it depends."

More than what? Suppose the question is rephrased as: "does a high-performance, green building that saves energy, water, and waste; contributes to good health and productivity of the occupants; and will last for 50 years cost more, initially, than the cheapest, minimally code-compliant structure that will be need to be replaced in 10 years?" In this case, the answer will be yes, absolutely. But if the comparison is between a green building and a building designed with quality and durability in mind, the first costs may not be that different. The baseline assumptions–what you are using to compare to the green building–are important factors in cost assessments.

More when? If one considers only the costs of the initial construction, a green building may cost more. But inherent in the idea of sustainability is a concern for the long-term effects of the building's construction and operation. The economics of sustainable buildings must include a calculation of life cycle costs–operating and maintenance costs as well as first costs. A properly designed green building will have lower energy and other utility costs. It will require less maintenance and will last longer, thus saving the owner money over the life of the building.

More to whom? This answer is different depending on who is paying. In some cases the building owner pays for the building, but passes the operating costs on to tenants. There are monetary and nonmonetary costs borne by building occupants as well as the local community. And what costs will the planet bear?

Asking the right cost question is an important concept in sustainable design. The common question, "how much more does a green building cost," carries the assumption that sustainable design strategies are optional accessories. Those with this attitude can fall into a trap of seeing green design as an "add-on" or unnecessary luxury, rather than as a different approach to design with a different set of values. As demonstrated by advocates of "integrated design," moving away from this "add-on" mode of thinking to a holistic view of building systems and performance is the best way to deliver a cost-effective, even cost-saving, green building.

LIFE-CYCLE COST APPROACHES

Life-cycle cost calculations factor in the cost of owning and operating a building as well as its initial design and construction. Figure 44 shows a simple life-cycle cost analysis used to select the mechanical system in a university residence hall. The three alternatives were 1) ground-source (geothermal) heat pumps, 2) four-pipe fan coil units with central boiler and chiller, and 3) individual "through-the-wall" packaged terminal air conditioner (PTAC) units. The top graph in figure 44 shows the initial construction costs for each. The through-the-wall units are the least expensive, and the other two alternatives are about equal. The lower graph in figure 44 shows the 25-year life-cycle costs that include energy use, maintenance, and replacement costs. Here, the geothermal system, because of its much lower fuel costs and lower maintenance requirements, has the lowest life-cycle cost by far. For a client like a university that pays for both first and long-term costs, that owns and operates its facilities, and that expects to use them for a long time, this analysis can be convincing.

This simple life cycle cost analysis does not, however, provide a guide to how much more we should pay up front to get the long-term benefits. This type of investment decision can be analyzed in several ways. An article in the *Journal of Green Building* provides an excellent overview of different financial calculations for comparing investments in green buildings (Wolff 2006). The article discusses several common financial analysis methods including simple payback, net present value, and internal rate of return. Using each of these methods, it analyzes examples of decisions about particular building components to illustrate the differing results.

FIGURE 44

Life Cycle Costs: The top graph compares the initial construction cost of three alternative HVAC systems. The lower graph shows the 20-year life-cycle cost of the same three systems. The system with the lowest initial cost does not have the lowest life-cycle cost. *Source: Alderson Engineering.*

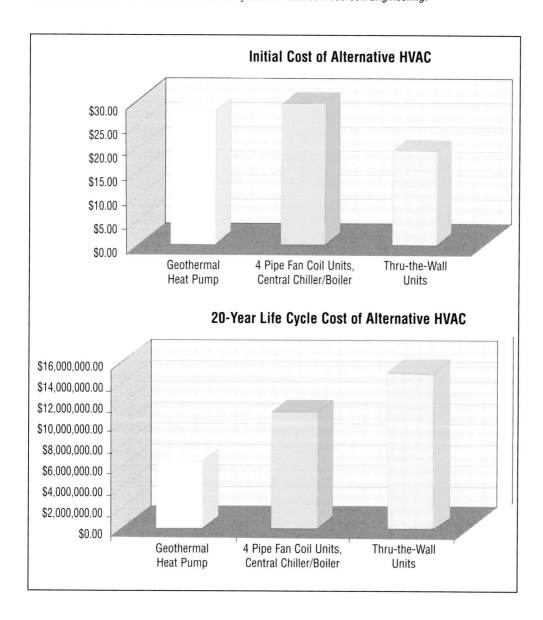

Simple Payback

Simple payback is a relatively straightforward calculation that many architects are familiar with. It is the ratio of the added cost of a feature divided by the expected annual savings benefit. Wolff uses the example of additional wall insulation that costs $1,500 more than the minimum required by building code. The annual saving in energy consumption is projected to be $93. The simple payback would be $1,500/$93 = 16 years. Many owners would consider this payback period too long and would not choose to make this investment.

But Wolff makes the point that simple payback does not consider several important factors that are often used to make decisions about investments. These include the expected inflation rate, the useful life of the green upgrade, and the rate of interest an investor would have to pay to borrow funds for the investment. Wolff reviews two other analysis methods, net present value (NPV) and internal rate of return (IRR), that do consider these "time factors" of money.

Net Present Value

NPV expresses life-cycle cost based on a set time horizon and considers the savings generated by the added feature as well as inflation, the cost of borrowing (discount rate), and the expected life of the investment. In Wolff's example of the added insulation, using assumptions about future increases in fuel prices, interest rates, and so on, the NPV of the added insulation ($4,500) is slightly lower, over a 30-year period, than the standard design ($4,714). This analysis suggests that this investment *is* worth making.

Internal Rate of Return

The IRR uses the same information from the NPV analysis, but is expressed in terms of "income" generated by the life-cycle savings from the additional investment. The unit for IRR is percent of the initial cost of the investment. For the added insulation, the 30-year IRR is seven percent. In other words, putting money into the higher insulation value is equivalent to an investment that earns seven percent, which can then be compared to the interest rates of alternative capital investments like certificates of deposit, savings bonds, bank accounts, mutual funds, or the stock market. If the IRR of a sustainable building is higher than other alternatives, it is a better investment.

TABLE 12

Three ways to analyze the value of investing in green building design. *Data source: Wolff, 2006.*

	Simple Payback			Net Present Value (NPV)		Internal Rate of Return (IRR)
	Incremental Capital Cost	First Year Financial Savings	Simple Payback	NPV of higher insulation	NPV of baseline insulation	IRR
Additional Wall Insulation	$1,500	$93	16.1	$25,100	$25,314	7%

Capital vs. Operating Expense

A significant barrier to some owners taking the life-cycle cost approach is the traditional separation of capital budgets from operating budgets. Not all owners can easily combine these, as required by life-cycle accounting. In many institutions and government agencies, for example, capital and operating expenses are accounted for in different budgets and often controlled by different departments. In other cases, the operating costs and construction costs may be paid by different entities. For example, a developer may own an office building and pay for its construction but then lease space to tenants who pay the operating expenses. In these cases, it may be difficult to use life-cycle costing arguments to justify investments in sustainable buildings without some form of incentive to offset the initial costs. In one innovative approach to solving this problem, Harvard University has developed a revolving loan fund from its capital budget that is used to invest in green building designs. The loans from the Harvard Green Campus Initiative are repaid from the operating budget through annual operating savings from lower energy and other costs (http://www.greencampus.harvard.edu/gclf/). Some private developers are also beginning to use these financial analysis tools. For instance, Daniel Jenkins, principal of the John Buck Company of Chicago says LEED can demonstrate to a tenant the anticipated long-term operating savings. "In turn, that enhances a building's image and can justify a higher rent." (U.S. Green Building Council 2006) This thinking is spreading to other speculative real estate developers.

FIRST COSTS

Although life-cycle costing may be needed to justify sustainable design, construction budgets are always important and cannot be ignored. Experienced design teams are producing high-performing green building designs with little or no added first cost by using *integrated design*, discussed in detail later. This is more common with large building projects. On small projects, however, it is not as easy to find cost trade-offs within the smaller budget.

There have been a number of studies analyzing the incremental cost of building green. Three prominent studies can be found on the Resources/Research section of the USGBC web site: the 2003 Capital E report to the California Sustainable Building Task Force, the 2004 U.S. General Services Administration (GSA) LEED Cost Study, and a 2004 paper by cost consulting firm Davis Langdon called Costing Green: A Comprehensive Cost Database and Budgeting Methodology. Each study uses a different approach to first-cost issues, but together they suggest a general consensus on costs and benefits.

CAPITAL E REPORT

The state of California has been a leader in the implementation of sustainable design in government facilities. The California Sustainable Building Task Force, an interagency committee, commissioned this study to investigate the costs of building green and to quantify the benefits (Kats 2003). Although the sample sizes are small, the comprehensive research methodology that went into establishing the benefits of sustainable design are as useful as the results themselves. The study has been called "the most definitive cost benefit analysis of green building ever conducted" and is cited frequently by sustainable design experts.

TABLE 13
Summary of benefits of green building from the Capital E study. *Source: Kats 2003.*

FINANCIAL BENEFITS OF GREEN BUILDINGS Summary	
Category	*20 yr. NPV*
Energy Savings	$5.80
Emissions Savings *(based on "market value")*	$1.20
Water Savings	$0.50
Operations & Maintenance Savings *(via Commissioning)*	$8.50
Productivity & Health Benefits *(1% increase for Certified & Silver, 1.5% for Gold & Platinum)*	$36.90 - $55.30
SUBTOTAL	$52.90 - $71.30
Average Extra Cost of Building Green	($3.00) – ($5.00)
TOTAL 20-year NET BENEFIT	$50.00 - $65.00

The Capital E study investigated construction cost data for 33 LEED-registered and -certified buildings that had been built or were nearing completion before 2003 in order to estimate the cost increase for green design. None of the buildings studied had been assigned a baseline value—the cost of a comparable "standard" building—so the report authors interviewed members of each project team to establish the cost premium, if any, that green building strategies added to each project. These were correlated with the level of the actual or anticipated LEED rating. For buildings expected to receive the lowest LEED rating, "certified," actual increased costs were only a little above the baseline (+0.66 percent). For buildings expected to receive the highest rating, Platinum, the increase of project costs over the baseline were the highest (+6.5 percent). The average increase for all 33 projects was just under two percent. This translates to an increase of $4 per square foot [$43/m²] for the average California construction cost of $200 per square foot [$2150/m²]. These figures have now become something of a rule-of-thumb for many in the industry, in spite of the small data set in this study.

One innovative aspect of the Capital E study is the thorough analysis of benefits provided by green buildings. While energy and water conservation can be relatively easily quantified and converted to cost savings, other alleged benefits of green building, from reductions of GHG emissions to productivity boosts for building occupants, are more elusive, and they resist easy translation into dollars. This study reviewed the research literature and developed a methodology to quantify, in life-cycle NPV costs, all of these benefits.

Energy Benefits

The Capital E study attempted to convert a number of the most important benefits of sustainable buildings into a 20-year life-cycle-cost NPV. The study assumed an average operational energy savings for LEED buildings of 30 percent better than code, based on data reported by USGBC and other sources. In addition, for commercial buildings, there is an added cost savings for a reduced peak electricity load, due to electricity rates that vary with time of day. In California, as in most regions, commercial power rates are designed to reward users of off-peak power and penalize peak-time users. This is because utility companies must use their least efficient, least profitable (and often most polluting) power plants during their highest demand time, typically on summer afternoons. While LEED does not directly address peak load management, the 33 buildings studied indicate that "green buildings provide reduction in peak demand." Using an average of California off-peak and peak rates with some conservative estimates of the potential peak reduction of green buildings, Capital E developed a projected annual savings for lowered peak demand. Adding together all these factors, the study calculates a 20-year NPV of $5.79 per square foot [$62.32/m²] for total energy savings in green buildings. Comparing this to the initial investment, or premium, of $4 per square foot [$43.06/m²] for the green building features suggests that green buildings are a good investment, based on energy savings alone.

Water Savings Benefits

Like energy savings, the value of water conservation is relatively straightforward to calculate and is, at least partly, based on the reduced cost paid to the water utility. The utility savings are based on average data from the USGBC suggesting that most green buildings save at least 30 percent on water consumption compared to a minimally code-compliant building. These water savings can be accomplished by simple, inexpensive measures such as drought-tolerant planting, high-efficiency irrigation, and low-flow plumbing fixtures. However, there are additional benefits to the public because of reduced demand on infrastructure and the avoided cost of not building additional water treatment systems, particularly in regions of the United States that are "water challenged." Using values for these avoided costs that were computed for other water economy studies, Capital E derives a NPV for water savings of $0.51 per square foot [$5.49/m²].

Waste Reduction Benefits

The Capital E study quantifies the benefits of reduced construction and demolition waste (encouraged in LEED by two potential points) by analyzing the avoided cost of sending debris to a landfill, which can be substantial, depending on the project location. In addition, there are other benefits to recycling or reuse. For example, the study cites analyses that show economic development benefits and avoided environmental costs for recycling rather than disposal. The study authors combine these approaches to simulate the benefits for construction of a typical California office building and to derive a relatively conservative 20-year NPV for reduced construction waste of $.03 per square foot [$0.32/m²].

CAPITAL E STUDY

A Report to California's Sustainable Building Task Force, October 2003

Energy Benefits

Green building energy savings primarily come from reduced electricity purchases, and secondarily from reduced peak energy demand. The financial benefits of 30 percent reduced consumption at an electricity price of $0.11 per kilowatt hour are about $0.44 per square feet per year [$4.74/m²], with a 20-year present value of $5.48 per square foot [$58.99/m²]. The additional value of peak demand reduction from green buildings is estimated at $0.025 per square foot per year [$0.27/m²], with 20-year present value of $0.31 per square foot [$3.34/m²]. Together, the total 20-year present value of financial energy benefits from a typical green building is $5.79 per square foot [$62.32/m²]. Thus, on the basis of energy savings alone, investing in green buildings appears to be cost-effective.

Emissions Benefits

The average California state building uses electricity at a rate of about 10 kilowatt hours per square foot per year. Converting this to Gigawatt hours (GWh) , multiplying by the [projected] emissions factors for 2010…and then multiplying again by the [recommended] prices per ton… yields yearly emissions costs per square foot… This report will assume… $5 per ton value of carbon, indicating a 20-year PV of $1.18 per square foot [$12.70/m²]for emissions reductions from green buildings.

Water Savings Benefits

Green buildings are designed to conserve water. Taking the avoided cost of water to be only the average retail price paid… to local utilities, the literature suggests that there is considerable potential for cost-effective water conservation strategies in new and renovated building projects in many regions of the state. However, the actual value of water conservation to the state is not the avoided cost of retail

continued on next page

water rates. Rather, it is the region-specific added cost of new marginal water supplies…[Combining these two cost savings] provides a 20-year PV of $0.51 per square foot [$5.49/m^2] for water savings from green buildings.

WASTE SAVINGS BENEFITS

It is possible, with a set of tentative assumptions, to estimate waste benefits associated with green buildings. This report uses the numbers from [several studies] to calculate rough conservative values for [construction and demolition] diversion for new construction as well as demolition of pre-existing structure before construction:

- $0.03 per square foot [$0.32/m^2] or $3,000 per 100,000-square-foot building for construction only.
- $0.14 per square foot [$1.51/m^2] or $14,000 per 100,000-square-foot building for construction preceded by demolition.

In the absence of good data on present rates of waste diversion in green and conventional buildings during both their construction and operation, it is impossible to quantify the relative advantages of either one. However, it appears probable that the green building waste reduction advantage would not exceed about $0.50 per square foot [$5.38/m^2], because of California's already aggressive waste reduction targets…

Commissioning and Operations & Maintenance (O&M) Benefits

Commissioning and metering contribute to lower [operations and maintenance] costs, such as extended equipment life, though how much lower is not known. O&M costs in state buildings–$3,039 per person per year or $12.25 per square foot per year [$131.86/m^2]–are nearly an order of magnitude larger than energy costs. Therefore any reduction in O&M costs has a significant impact on financial benefits. For example, a reduction in O&M costs of 10 percent is equal to a savings of $304 per person, or

continued on next page

Emissions Benefits

When it comes to estimating emissions, the study departs from the relatively easily quantified benefits. There is certainly an ecological benefit to reducing GHG emissions, but there is no accepted method for converting this pollution prevention into a monetary benefit. GHG emission "credits" are actually traded as a commodity through a robust, international exchange in Europe. In the United States, where there are as yet few emissions restrictions, there is only a small market. U.S. trade prices for these credits have a wide range–from less than $1 to over $16 per ton of CO_2. Based on a review of trading price data and of other studies that sought to establish a cost for emissions, the Capital E study uses a conservatively low, but nonetheless arbitrary rate of $5 per ton ($CO_2$) for the reduction of carbon through green building energy savings. This adds an additional $1.18 to the 20-year NPV.

Benefits from Commissioning

Basic building systems commissioning is a prerequisite for LEED certification. This generally involves an additional inspection of the construction and initial operational start-up of HVAC and other critical equipment. There is growing evidence that commissioning provides both short-term and long-term benefits to building owners through improved performance and lower maintenance costs. Capital E cites several studies suggesting that "savings from commissioning exceeded the cost of commissioning even before the projects were complete." These savings accrued because commissioning:

- Helped eliminate costly change orders
- Reduced requests for cost information
- Helped ensure proper system/component selection
- Improved performance of building systems
- Reduced call backs

Based on these benefits and the results from several other sources, the study establishes a somewhat arbitrary but conservative (low) estimate of five percent annual savings on O&M. Based on average O&M costs for California state buildings, this results in a 20-year NPV of $8.47.

Health & Productivity Benefits

There is growing evidence, in peer-reviewed studies, of the health and productivity benefits of many green-building features such as natural lighting, views, and improved indoor air quality. Capital E cites many of these studies in their report and concludes that "four of the attributes associated with green building design–increased ventilation control, increased temperature control, increased lighting control, and increased daylighting–have been positively and significantly correlated with increased productivity. Additionally, there is a large range in potential productivity and health gains from improved indoor environmental quality." In spite of this, few of the studies have attempted to assign a value to the expected benefit in productivity gains or lower absenteeism. Based on their review of the literature, Capital E recommends a one-percent productivity increase for LEED-Certified and Silver buildings and a 1.5 percent gain for Gold and Platinum. These numbers are relatively arbitrary, but generally supported by the studies. This seemingly small percentage increase in productivity translates into an enormous savings when multiplied by labor costs. These calculations show a 20-year NPV of $36.89 per square foot [$397.08/m²] for Certified and Silver-level buildings, and $55.33 per square foot [$595.57/m²] for Gold- and Platinum-level buildings.

Conclusions

Many observers have noted that productivity and health benefits attributed to green buildings may greatly outweigh the building systems' operational savings based on annual and life-cycle costs. This study's conclusions certainly support that assertion. The strength of the study lies in the care and rigor that went into the attempt to quantify cost savings for a wide variety of benefits, some of which are derived from subjective qualities that are difficult to measure. The study's main weaknesses are the size of the data set and the many seemingly arbitrary decisions made to generate the final cost savings. However, even if one questions the report's assumptions on health and productivity benefits or the value placed on avoided GHG emissions, making these figures still lower and more conservative would not change the conclusion. The study shows that green buildings do make economic sense on a life-cycle basis, particularly for a government entity or institution that builds for the long term, even ignoring the less quantifiable benefits.

GSA LEED COST STUDY

Document PBS-P100, 2003, Facilities Standards for the Public Buildings Service of the GSA identifies sustainability and energy performance as basic tenets of their general design philosophy. The P100 document also specifically refers to LEED and requires all new construction and major renovation and modernization projects to be LEED-certified, with a recommended Silver level. Given the

$1.35 per square foot per year [$14.53/m²]. There is not enough data to estimate with any precision the reduction in O&M costs that would occur in green buildings. Clearly the reduction is larger than zero but probably under 25 percent. To be conservative, this report assumes that green buildings experience an O&M cost decline of 5 percent per year. This equals a savings of $0.68 per square foot per year[$7.32/m²], for a 20-year PV savings of $8.47 per square foot [$91.17/m²].

Productivity & Health Benefits

Given the studies and data reviewed… this report recommends attributing a one-percent productivity and health gain to certified and Silver-level buildings and a 1.5 percent gain to Gold- and Platinum-level buildings. These percentages are at the low end of the range of productivity gains for each of the individual specific building measures–ventilation, thermal control, light control, and daylighting–analyzed above. They are consistent with or well below the range of [the] additional studies cited above.

For State of California employees, a one-percent increase in productivity (equal to about 5 minutes per working day) is equal to $665 per employee per year, or $2.96 per square foot per year[$31.86/m²]. A 1.5 percent increase in productivity (or a little over 7 minutes each working day) is equal to $998 per year, or $4.44 per square foot per year [$47.79/m²]. At $4.44 per year, over 20 years, and at a 5 percent discount rate (assuming that state employee salaries are unchanged with respect to inflation), the PV of the productivity benefits is about $36.89 per square foot [$397.08/m²] for certified and Silver-level buildings, and $55.33 per square foot [$595.57/m²] for Gold- and Platinum-level buildings. Assuming a longer building operational life, such as 30 or 40 years, would result in substantially larger benefits.

Source: The Costs and Financial Benefits of Green Buildings: A Report to California's Sustainable Building Task Force, October 2003, principal author: Greg Kats, Capital E.

size of the GSA portfolio—over 8,300 facilities housing over one million federal employees—the effect of these policies will be enormous. As these standards were being implemented in 2003, the agency commissioned a study to analyze the implications of LEED on project costs.

This study, conducted by Steven Winter & Associates (SWA), focused exclusively on first costs, both hard and soft, and looked at two of the most common GSA construction projects, a new mid-rise federal courthouse and a mid-rise federal office building renovation/ modernization. The methodology for this study was to begin with detailed prototype designs that GSA had already prepared for budget modeling. These prototypes were based on earlier GSA standards, before the implementation of the LEED requirement. SWA developed alternate designs and budgets that would achieve LEED-Certified, Silver, and Gold levels for both the courthouse and office renovation projects.

Each prototype design was assumed to be located in downtown Washington, DC. A low-cost and high-cost version for each LEED rating level was developed to provide a range of costs to allow for variations between regions, climate, and other conditions, so that the results would be applicable in locales across the United States. For the office renovation, the two scenarios were based on either a "minimal" or a "full" façade renovation, a scope decision that has a significant effect on overall projects costs, and, not incidentally, potential LEED credit attainment.

The study also looked at the "LEED-related" soft costs for each level of rating. These soft costs included design cost premiums for any tasks that would increase the team's scope of work during design and construction, plus those tasks associated with

FIGURE 45
LEED-NC Certified Annex Building for Social Security Administration Woodlawn, MD. *Source: General Services Administration.*

documenting and submitting a LEED application to the USGBC. The overall design fees were assumed to be a percentage of construction costs, so if total costs rose, the total fee would go up too. This fee increase was in addition to the estimated compensation for any specific tasks identified as beyond standard design services, but required for the specific level of LEED rating, such as charrette facilitation or energy analysis.

GSA Standards

It is important to note that the GSA design-and-construction standards were already quite high before the addition of LEED requirements. For example, GSA had set energy performance targets for their projects above code, using energy use intensities

(Btu per square foot per year [kW/m²/yr]). For the new courthouse, the target range was 45-50 kBtu per square foot per year [130-145 kW/m²/yr], a level that would be a 14 percent improvement over code and provide one LEED point. For the office renovation, the target of 50-55 kBtu per square foot per year [145-160 kW/m²/yr] would be a 14-18 percent improvement and score two or three LEED points. Because these were already GSA standards, no cost was attributed to these levels of attainment. However, if additional energy performance were required to reach higher levels of LEED rating, costs for implementing the strategies to achieve the higher levels was added.

For design costs, GSA already required building commissioning, which is a prerequisite in LEED, so no added soft costs were assumed for this task. In addition, GSA required a base level of energy modeling for their projects. The study assumed that the GSA-mandated energy consulting was sufficient for Certified and Silver ratings, and no added design costs were attributed to this task. To achieve LEED Gold, however, augmented energy analysis was assumed, and estimated design costs were added for these services.

Conclusions

The results of the GSA study are shown in figure 46. For the new courthouse building, construction costs for a LEED rating ranged considerably. The lowest level of LEED, Certified, actually resulted in a *savings* of $0.76 per square foot [$8.18/m²]. This savings derives principally from eliminating site work such as an irrigation system to achieve LEED credits. The higher Gold rating showed an increase cost of $17.70 per square foot [$190.52/m²]. For the office building renovation project, added costs ranged from $1.78 per square foot [$19.16/m²] for LEED Certified to $10.58 per square foot [$113.88/m²]for LEED Gold. In both cases, a LEED Silver rating, recommended as the minimum in the GSA standards document, was determined to be achievable for an approximately four percent higher construction cost, somewhat higher than the findings of the California report. This study also identified several "synergistic credits," or combinations of strategies that help a project earn multiple LEED points for less cost than achieving them individually.

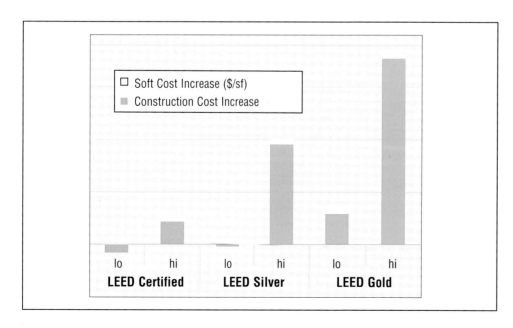

FIGURE 46

Added cost of LEED and green features from the Capital E study for the state of California. *Source: Kats 2003.*

DAVIS LANGDON COST STUDY

A third cost study, also focused on first costs only, was conducted by Davis Langdon, an international construction cost consulting company with offices around the world (http://www.davislangdon.com/). The size of Davis Langdon enabled them to assemble a large database of costs for a variety of projects. For this study, they looked at their database of costs for several building types to compare projects seeking LEED certification with those that did not. The types analyzed in the study were libraries, laboratories, and college classroom buildings. The results, shown in figures 47A, B, and C, are very revealing. In each case, there was no correlation between the overall construction cost of LEED and non-LEED buildings, nor between the level of LEED and first cost. There were low-cost green buildings and high-cost green buildings; there were low-cost nongreen buildings and high-cost nongreen buildings.

The study authors caution against making strong conclusions on the basis of their data because of the small data set and the wide range of construction costs within each building type. Nonetheless, Davis Langdon writes, "a majority of the buildings studied were able to achieve their goals for LEED certification without any additional funding… From this analysis we can conclude that many projects can achieve sustainable design within their initial budget, or with very small supplemental funding." This suggests that owners are finding ways to incorporate the elements

FIGURE 47A

A comparison of LEED and non-LEED buildings of similar building types shows there is no correlation between higher levels of LEED certification and higher costs. *Source: Davis Langdon.*

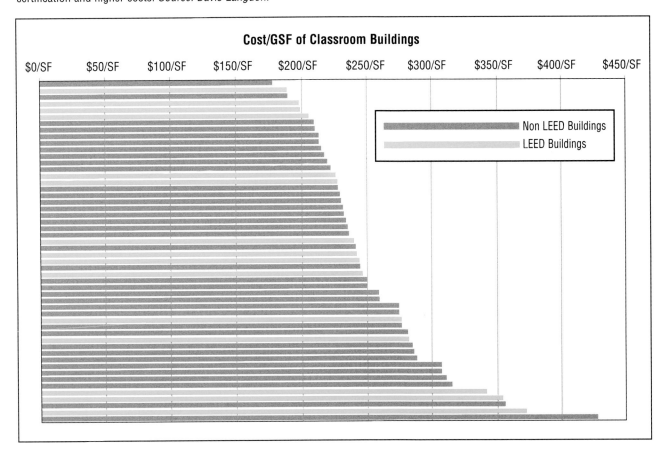

FIGURE 47B

A comparison of LEED and non-LEED libraries. *Source: Davis Langdon.*

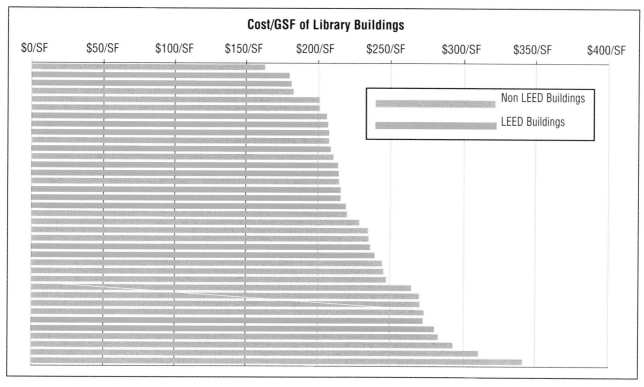

FIGURE 47C

A comparison of LEED and non-LEED laboratories. *Source: Davis Langdon.*

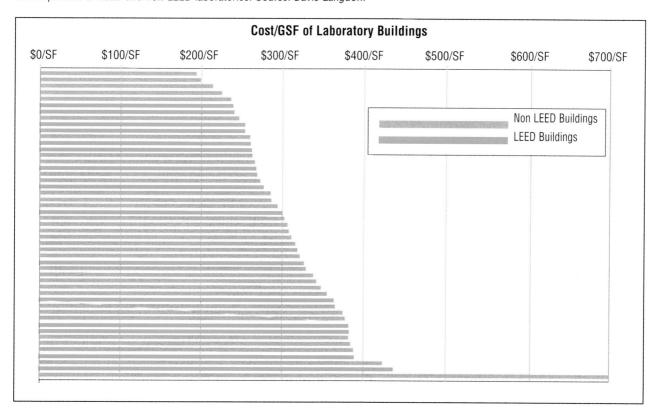

important to the goals and values of the project, regardless of budget, by making choices and value decisions.

DO GREEN BUILDINGS COST MORE?
Based on these three studies, the answer is, "yes and no." The evidence suggests that there may be an initial cost premium to be paid, for both design and construction costs, to achieve higher-performing green buildings. However, the evidence also shows that the long-term benefits to owners, occupants, society, and the planet are substantial and provide demonstrated economic and ecological rewards that should not be ignored. Experience has also shown that when sustainable design is incorporated into the project goals from the beginning, through an integrated design process, the budget will more easily accommodate higher performance with little or no added cost.

SUSTAINABLE DESIGN II

INTEGRATED DESIGN

Sustainability metrics and building rating systems are tools that can help architects produce high-performance green buildings. Experienced practitioners have found, however, that successfully adopting these tools requires some adjustments to their standard design processes. The approach known as "whole-building design" or "integrated design" front-loads the design process with interdisciplinary collaboration, approaches the building as an interactive system, and sets measurable performance goals.

What is Integrated Building Design?

The goal of integrated design is to create a high-performance building, one that optimizes form, function, time, economics, and environmental resources. Traditional building design typically treats environmental considerations as incidental rather than integral components.

Integrated building design considers relationships among building systems at a variety of scales. Building-scale design integration may involve assessing the effect of roofing-material selection on stormwater runoff volumes, for instance, while project-scale integration could address specific energy or economic goals. Community-scale design integration may focus on whether or how much the building requires increases in utility capacity or transportation routes. Optimizing design requires architects to carefully consider all integrated-design criteria. If one

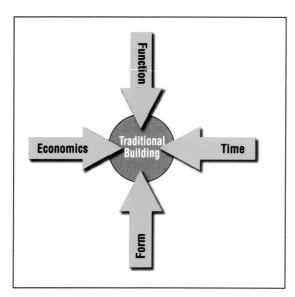

FIGURE 48A
Traditional design criteria. *Source: RMI.*

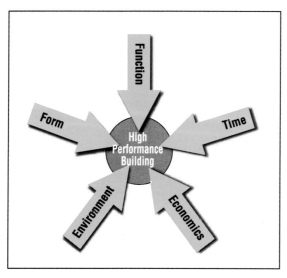

FIGURE 48B
Integrated-design criteria include environmental considerations. *Source: RMI.*

principle is neglected, the project may be less successful. Furthermore, all criteria must be discussed at the outset, when design decisions have the greatest influence on life-cycle building performance. A successful example of integrated design is the Natural Energy Laboratory of Hawaii.

Integrated design enables the design team to find ways to address multiple problems with single solutions. In the NELHA example, the carefully designed seawater system provided both space cooling and irrigation. For a tract-house project in Davis, California, synergies were exploited between window performance and the HVAC system. High-performance windows produced significant energy savings but had a higher first cost. When considered in isolation, the extra cost of the better windows appeared prohibitively expensive. An energy analysis indicated that the higher-performing windows decreased the heating load sufficiently to downsize the furnace. When coupled with the cost savings of the smaller HVAC system, the more expensive windows actually *decreased* the overall first cost of the project (Rocky Mountain Institute 1997).

The Hawaii research lab and Davis tract house are very different from each other, yet both are examples of successfully applying the five integrated-design criteria. While adding design criteria and incorporating whole-system thinking into one's customary process may seem daunting or unfamiliar, success depends more on com-

---

NATURAL ENERGY LABORATORY OF HAWAII AUTHORITY (NELHA)

The 3,600-square-foot [335-m^2] Hawaii Gateway Energy Center houses multipurpose space for displays, outreach, conferencing, and education. A 20-kilowatt photovoltaic array is mounted on signature space frames that extend above the visitor center on the north and serve as walkway canopies on the south. The calculated peak demand for the visitor center is approximately 10 kilowatts, making the center a net exporter of power. This unique facility has access to 43-degree Fahrenheit [6°C] seawater pumped from 3,000 feet [915 meters] below sea level; the cool water is used to passively condition the building. Outside air is drawn over cooling coils and circulated through the space, and the water that condenses on the coils is used for landscaping irrigation and toilet flushing. The center is entirely naturally illuminated during daylight hours, thanks to its north-south orientation.

FIGURE 49

Natural Energy Laboratory of Hawaii. *Photo by Victor Olgyay, courtesy RMI.*

mitment than innovation. Creating a high-performance project will require more time and effort at the beginning of the process than designing a conventional building. Many teams find, however, that this early investment of design time is rewarded by a more coordinated project as the documentation progresses. Careful coordination among project participants, making decisions with the long term in mind, and learning from past mistakes all simplify the integrated-design process.

Integrated-Design Participants

The integrated-design team must include a variety of disciplines appropriate for the requirements of the project. Just as important as individual skill sets is the attitude each member brings to the team. An open mind in considering the perspectives of other disciplines is crucial. Architects must be open to input from engineers and other consultants on building design decisions, and vice versa.

It is important to include the general contractor or construction manager if at all possible. As the cost and constructability expert, the builder can provide vital strategic feedback during the integrated-design process, and his or her "buy-in" is crucial to ensure the project goals are realized as the building moves into construction.

It is also useful to identify a project "champion," someone who acts as both a facilitator and a sustainability advocate. The champion may be from any profession and serve additional roles on the project team. Pinpointing one team member to guide the integrated-design process is a key to success.

Involving all team members from the outset is yet another important component of integrated design. Up to 70 percent of a building's life-cycle costs may be determined when less than 1 percent of up-front costs have been spent (Romm 1994). The most important decisions are made on the first day (Hawken, Lovins, and Lovins 1999).

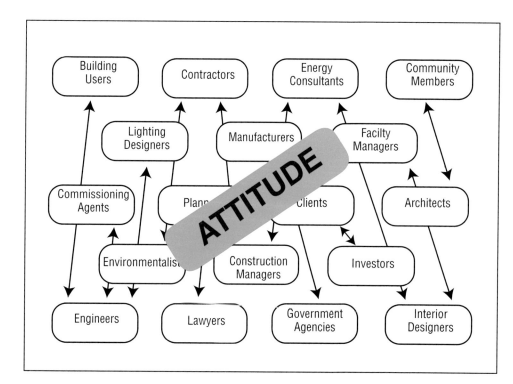

FIGURE 50

Just as important as individual skill sets is the attitude each member brings to the team. An open mind in considering the perspectives of other disciplines is crucial. *Source: RMI.*

FIGURE 51

The most effective time to consider environmental factors is early in the design process. *Source: RMI.*

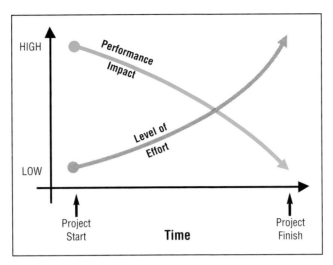

FIGURE 52

The traditional design process. *Source: RMI.*

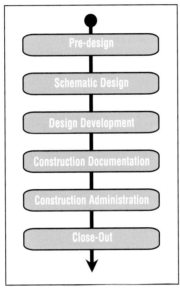

FIGURE 53

The integrated design process. *Source: RMI.*

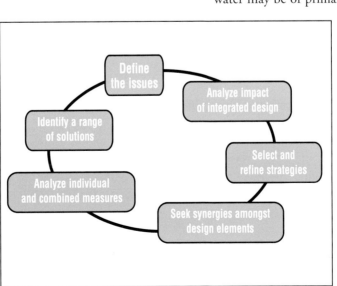

Integrated-Design Process

Integrated design is nonlinear and continuous, and thus is composed mostly of strategies rather than defined phases. Two key differences between conventional and integrated-design processes are the perceived duration of the project and the level of team commitment required. While a conventional building is considered complete upon occupancy, a high-performance building is ideally never finished. By definition, a high-performing structure must remain high performing! This insight implies a need for thoughtful planning and continued building monitoring and updating.

Integrated-design strategies must cover the entire lifetime of the building and account for activities that help the building adapt to environmental or programmatic changes. Figures 52 and 53 highlight the different segments and activities for both traditional and integrated-design processes.

Define the Issues

As detailed in figure 53, the first step in integrated design is to understand and define the critical issues. For a project in Phoenix, AZ, water may be of primary concern, while in California, energy may take center stage. An initial analysis of the project requirements, together with site, ecological, and climatic conditions, provides a necessary starting point from which to begin integrated design. As an example, energy use for a typical office building in Denver, CO is shown in figure 54. The dominant loads are lighting, cooling, and heating. This information can be used from the earliest stages of design to set targets and look for synergies, such as the interrelationships between building envelope and energy performance.

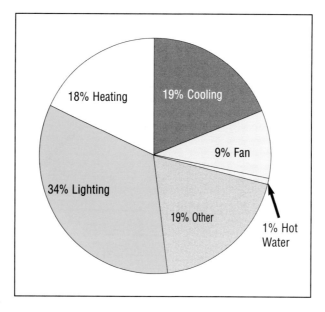

FIGURE 54
Annual energy operating costs for a Denver office building. *Source: RMI.*

Identify a Range of Solutions

After identifying the key issues, the design team should conduct a charrette or other collaborative brainstorming session to generate design alternatives. The five design criteria—form, function, cost, time, and environment—should drive the discussion. Typical areas to investigate for integrated-design opportunities include materials, stormwater, wastewater treatment, office equipment, and energy integration. Integrated-design ideas might include the use of captured rainwater for flushing toilets, the installation of smart building controls, or the selection of LCD over CRT computer monitors. All these strategies involve cost and performance trade-offs that may cost-effectively reduce the overall environmental impact.

Use Appropriate Metrics

Selecting the right metric to compare design alternatives is important. Sometimes one strategy can be evaluated using several different metrics. In the Denver office building example, annual energy cost was used to help make decisions about efficiency strategies. The base case (standard, code-minimum design) annual energy cost was $7,600. Figure 55 shows results from energy-simulation software indicating that daylighting and glazing upgrades would reduce the annual operating cost by 21 percent and 17 percent, respectively, compared to the base case.

Another way to compare design measures is to list the cost, savings, and simple payback period. This method is shown in Table 14.

Seek Synergies between Systems and Components

A key concept of integrated design is that looking at individual components does not reveal the whole story. To reduce costs and improve whole-building performance, it is imperative to look for synergies among systems. Optimizing individual components in isolation often has unintended consequences. If the systems are not designed to work together, they can end up working against each other. "The greater degree to which the components of a system are optimized together, the more the trade-offs and compromises that seem inevitable at the individual component level become unnecessary" (Hawken, Lovins, and Lovins 1999). Figure 56 demonstrates the savings that are achievable when several efficient design strategies are combined.

TABLE 14

Capital cost, annual savings, and payback period of individual building elements. *Source: RMI.*

ENERGY MEASURE	COST ($)	SAVINGS ($)	PAYBACK PERIOD (years)
Insulation	$1,600	$101	15.84
Economizer	$1,200	$165	7.27
Shading	$4,800	$325	14.77
HVAC Controls	$2,900	$506	5.73
Efficient HVAC	$3,880	$739	5.25
Efficient Lighting	$1,400	$860	1.63
Glazing	$5,520	$1,321	4.18
Daylighting	$4,900	$1,560	3.14

Select and Refine Strategies

Once the team has analyzed individual strategies and identified the synergies of selected combinations, the choice of design strategies and components is easier. Systems that best fit the five design criteria should be selected. Making these decisions may require updating energy models and further optimizing the various combinations of systems.

Another important concept of integrated design has been phrased: "tunneling through the cost barrier (RMI 1997)." This notion recognizes that in whole-system design, it is often possible to move past the standard "cost effectiveness limit"

FIGURE 55

Cost savings for individual building elements. *Source: RMI.*

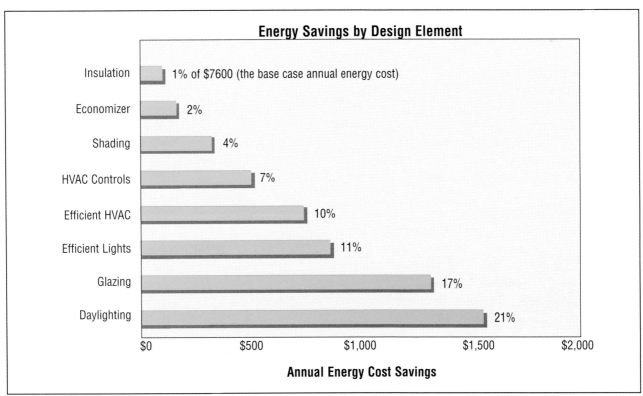

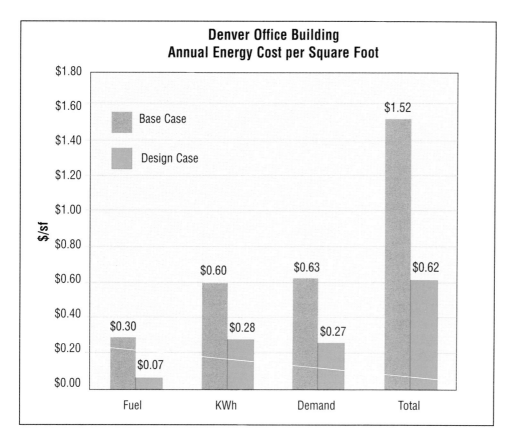

FIGURE 56

Base case compared to design case annual energy costs in a Denver office building.
Source: RMI.

of incremental improvements and realize bigger energy savings with less expensive first costs. A typical example is installing more insulation and better windows to reduce HVAC system size. A little more insulation or slightly better windows will result in a small increment of energy savings. A standard decision process might calculate a simple payback and stop there. However, the interaction between insulation and the required furnace or boiler size may mean that adding even more insulation the system can be downsized to the next smaller, and less expensive, model, thus offsetting the increased cost of the insulation and windows. Figure 57 illustrates the principle.

Analyze the Results

Once strategies have been selected, the new "design case" building can be compared to the "base case" to evaluate the performance with respect to the project goals. For the Denver office building example, the total savings compared to the additional cost are shown in Table 15.

After the design is complete, LEED-required commissioning

WHOLE BUILDING ANALYSIS	
Added Cost of Design Case:	$26,200
Reduced Cost of Design Case:	$21,860
Incremental Construction Cost:	$4,340
Energy Savings of Design Case:	$4,500/year
Simple Payback:	1 year +/-
Return on Investment:	100% +/-

TABLE 15

Whole-building costs.
Source: RMI.

helps ensure design goals are met during construction. Furthermore, tenants and building managers should be trained to monitor and report on building perform-

FIGURE 57

Tunneling through the cost barrier. *Source: RMI.*

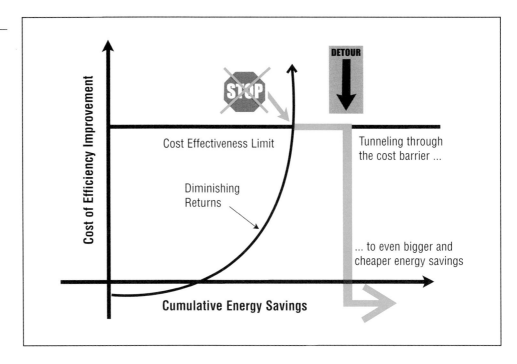

ance. Without such feedback, it is not possible to determine whether the project goals are actually achieved.

Integrated design, like whole-system engineering, is iterative and elaborate. Not formulaic, the process forces the design team to rethink the purpose of building components. As a constantly evolving process, it is an opportunity to improve on traditional design development.

Resources and Tools

There is a growing number of resources and tools that aid integrated design, ranging from design practices to energy modeling programs.

The design charrette is an "intensive workshop that enables design teams to use whole-system thinking to explore the interconnections among such elements as restorative site development, innovative energy-saving design and engineering, creative functional design concepts, worker productivity enhancements, and strategies to improve environmental sensitivity in design and construction." (www.rmi.org/sitepages/pid201.php) Typically a day or more in length, this facilitated event brings together multiple stakeholders and designers to set goals, articulate concerns, and generate ideas. The outcome of a charrette is not necessarily solutions, but rather identification and team consensus on key issues and aspirations. A detailed charrette handbook is available from the National Renewable Energy Laboratory. (www.eere.energy.gov)

The Whole Building Design Guide is published by the National Institute of Building Sciences (NIBS) and funded by the Naval Facility Engineering Command's Engineering Innovation and Criteria Office, the GSA, U.S. DOE, and the Sustainable Buildings Industry Council. It is "the only web-based portal providing government and industry practitioners with one-stop access to up-to-date information on a wide range of building-related guidance, criteria, and technology from a 'whole buildings' perspective." (www.wbdg.org)

Through the Office of Energy Efficiency and Renewable Energy's (EERE) Building Technologies Program, the DOE collaborates with numerous building industry professionals on energy-efficient technologies and design strategies. The Building Technologies Program supports eight main program areas, including the High Performance Buildings Program and the Building America program. The High Performance Building program focuses on commercial buildings and sponsors the High Performance Buildings Initiative, which aims to improve the energy efficiency of commercial buildings in the United States. The Building America program focuses on reducing energy consumption in residential buildings. The High Performance Buildings Initiative also sponsors the High Performance Buildings Database (www.eere.energy.gov/buildings/highperformance).

NREL, the nation's leading facility for renewable energy and energy efficiency research, is responsible for much of the research and development contained in the both the High Performance Building Program and the Building America program hosted by the DOE (www.nrel.gov/buildings).

EnergyPlus is a stand-alone energy simulation program used to model building energy flows including heating, cooling, lighting, and ventilating systems. Based on programs like BLAST and DOE-2, EnergyPlus gains more innovative simulation capabilities with each version. Features include the ability to model time increments of less than an hour, multizone air flow, displacement ventilation, and photovoltaic and solar thermal systems. EnergyPlus does not have a "user friendly" graphical interface. Instead, it reads input and writes output as text files, but numerous user interfaces and add-ons are currently available and under development (www.eere.energy.gov/buildings/energyplus).

Energy-10™ is an energy simulation tool that analyzes energy and cost savings achievable through the application of various sustainable design strategies. The software was developed in a collaborative effort by the NREL Center for Building and Thermal Systems, the Sustainable Buildings Industry Council, Lawrence Berkeley National Laboratory, and the Berkeley Solar Group. With relatively little input, Energy-10 can produce an accurate whole-building analysis of thermal, HVAC, and daylighting performance over an entire year. Best used for buildings with few thermal zones, Energy-10 is useful in compiling models early in design (www.sbicouncil.org).

DOE-2, primarily developed by Lawrence Berkeley National Laboratory and Hirsch & Associates, has been used to develop state, national, local, and international building-energy efficiency standards including ASHRAE 90.1. The program is useful for both detailed and rigorous energy conservation and building design studies. Inputs to the program include weather data, a description of the building and its HVAC system, and the utility rate structure. The unaltered DOE-2 program is a "DOS box" program, which requires much experience to operate effectively, though it gives seasoned users great flexibility (www.doe2.com).

eQUEST® is an interactive Windows implementation of DOE-2 with graphic displays. Still a sophisticated program, eQUEST allows designers without significant modeling experience to perform detailed comparative analyses of building designs. Three design aids, the "schematic wizard," the "design development wizard," and the "energy efficiency measure wizard," help overcome barriers to using DOE-2. eQUEST, the "Quick Energy Simulation Tool," is available free of cost from the State of California's Energy Design Resources program (www.energydesignresources.com).

INTEGRATED-DESIGN CASE STUDY

The Missouri Department of Natural Resources (MoDNR) building, formally named the Lewis and Clark State Office Building, is located in Jefferson City, MO. With four stories and 120,000 square feet [11,000-m²] of office space, the structure houses more than 400 state employees. As the first LEED Platinum-certified government building in the United States, the project was designed to serve as a model for future government projects. Additionally, the building was designed to be pedagogical, so equipment has been left exposed where possible, along with explanatory displays where appropriate, to explain the building's green features and functions to occupants and visitors.

The project design team was led by the Kansas City office of BNIM Architects and included Clanton Associates (lighting design), Conservation Design Forum (landscape), and RMI (daylighting and energy).

Project Features

Although energy receives much of the attention in integrated design, it is not the only important element. Integrated design must examine all project elements to ensure the optimization of each of the five design criteria. For the MoDNR building, the principles of integrated design were applied to siting, water management, materials selection, air distribution, and daylighting. The contributions of each of these, taken one at a time, are difficult to quantify, yet when combined in an energy model and whole-building analysis, the benefits are undeniable.

Integrated design begins with careful site selection. For the MoDNR building, the site was part of the Missouri State Penitentiary redevelopment project, in which a prison building had been taken down. A restorative landscape plan was implemented to enhance native ecosystems and to manage stormwater on the neglected and disturbed site.

One of the major goals for the MoDNR project was to eliminate stormwater runoff. Several innovative tactics were combined to achieve this goal. One component of the stormwater control initiative is a 50,000-gallon [190,000-liter] storage tank that collects roof runoff—this water will provide 95 percent of the building's gray-water needs. Another large component of the plan is site-retention devices including bioswales, detention ponds, and pervious paving. These measures

FIGURE 58

South side of the Missouri Department of Natural Resources (MoDNR) Lewis and Clark State Office Building. *Photo copyright © 2005 Mike Sinclair, Photographer, courtesy of BNIM Architects.*

should control runoff in all but the most intense storms.

Other water-related measures incorporated in the project include the installation of waterless urinals and low-flow fixtures. The landscaping also features local and native plants that do not require watering or mowing; this reduces not only water consumption, but maintenance and labor costs.

The MoDNR project took advantage of locally available and recycled materials where appropriate. Wood flooring came from a sustainable Missouri forest, and outdoor amenities, including benches and walkways, incorporated bricks from demolished buildings. The concrete used in the project contained 25 percent fly ash substituting for Portland cement, and 75 percent of all materials came from regional manufacturers. The decision to use a raised-floor system in the MoDNR building has numerous integrated-design benefits. First, a raised floor allows for under-floor air distribution, providing air to occupants via diffusers in the flooring panels. Because conditioned air is delivered from below, it is more efficient than a fully-mixing overhead system. Furthermore, an under-floor system provides better air quality and allows for greater occupant control. A second benefit to a raised floor is accessibility and flexibility. It is easier to remove one carpet panel to fix an Internet cable, for instance, than to perch on a ladder and remove ceiling tiles. And third, a raised floor system covers the cabling, ducts, and other equipment often concealed above a dropped ceiling. In the MoDNR building, the ceilings were left exposed and painted a reflective color to help distribute daylight.

To maximize the benefits of sunlight, the MoDNR building is equipped with the latest daylighting technologies, electrical lighting systems, and control equipment. Because lighting and the associated cooling loads are major energy users in office buildings, daylighting drove many of the architectural decisions including the orientation and massing of the structure. The long elevations of the building face north and south, a configuration that is ideal for daylighting. The building has a narrow cross section, 75 feet [22.9 meters] at a maximum, so that no point in the interior is more than 38 feet [11.6 meters] from a window.

Two high-efficiency glazing products were used for the windows. One has a visible transmittance of 70 percent and a solar heat gain coefficient (SHGC) of 0.357; the second assembly has a transmittance of 60 percent and an SHGC of 0.3. These high-performance glazing systems are optimized for different solar orientations by maximizing the visible light transmittance while minimizing the solar heat gain. The overall U-value of the fenestration is 0.425, exceeding that required by code by 28 percent.

The exterior of the south face of the building features precast concrete vertical fins and horizontal light shelves. These components shade the structure from extreme summer sun yet reflect diffuse daylight deep into the building. Interior fabric light shelves further bounce light into the core, reducing the need for electrical lighting. Daylight occupancy sensors control the high-efficiency electric lighting to ensure that potential energy savings are actually realized. Also, daylighting and electric lighting are both designed to control glare to reduce eyestrain and improve occupant comfort and productivity.

Energy Analysis

Energy analysis is critical to the design of an integrated building because it enables the benefits of design synergies to be quantified. For example, it is only possible to accurately predict the energy savings effects of different building orientations through an energy model.

The following simplified example uses Energy-10 outputs to illustrate the role of energy analysis in integrated design. This simulation tool analyzes energy and cost savings achievable through the application of various sustainable design strategies. Energy-10 is useful for architects during an early phase of design to help them determine which sustainable strategies are most appropriate for the project.

The first step in developing any energy model is to correctly define the inputs. Designers or their energy consultants should be familiar with the analysis tools and understand how they calculate their outputs. A helpful "big picture" metric is annual energy use intensity. Analyzing the annual energy use by function—heating, lighting, and so on—is useful to begin understanding relationships within the building.

Figure 59 details annual energy use for the MoDNR building. While a comparable high-energy-consuming (base case) building uses 74,800 Btu per square foot [219,000 kW/m²], the low-energy-consuming (design case) building uses only 42,900 [126,000 kW/m²]. The largest load in both cases is heating while the smallest is cooling.

To generate the annual energy use, it is first necessary to define and understand characteristics of and interactions among the various building components. For this example, we focus on the HVAC and lighting-system outputs.

The HVAC hour-by-hour outputs help characterize the heating and cooling loads shown in the Annual Energy Use graph. Changing the building layout, window area, glazing characteristics, system efficiencies, internal loads, lighting loads, and building schedules can all significantly affect heating and cooling loads. Tweaking these inputs and understanding their effects on whole-building performance is essential to successfully optimize building performance.

FIGURE 59

Annual energy use in the MoDNR Lewis and Clark State Office Building. *Source: RMI.*

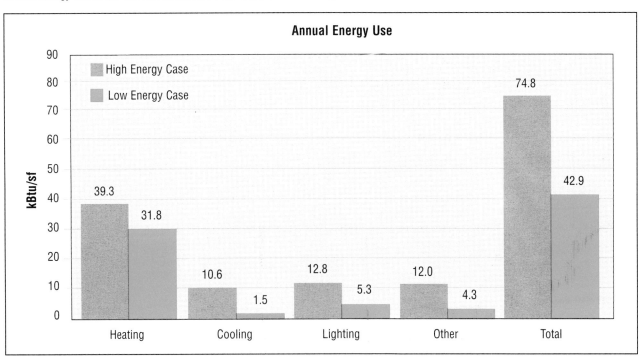

Figures 60A and 60B show the heating and cooling loads for the MoDNR building during a typical day in January and a day in July. For the high-energy case in January (figure 60A), the building has high heating loads at night and much lower loads during the day. The low-energy case has a much more stable profile, with low loads throughout both the day and night. It is not surprising that the high-energy case consumes more total energy than the low-energy case due to less insulation, lower system efficiencies, and inefficient windows. But it may at first seem unexpected that the high-energy case has lower loads during the day. The unintended consequence of using less-efficient lighting becomes an apparent benefit in the high-energy case, reducing the heating load during the day.

Not surprisingly, the loads for the July day (figure 60B) are much different from those observed in January. Again, the low-energy case, at around 100 kBtu [29kWh] is much more stable than the high-energy case, which dramatically peaks at nearly 400 kBtu [116 kWh]. Furthermore, this cooling season peak occurs in the late afternoon when the electric utilities are typically experiencing their greatest demand and rates are the highest. Taking into account not only the quantity of energy consumed but also the timing of the peaks is essential to reducing costs.

The lighting-energy profiles (figures 61A and 61B) tell a similar story to those of the HVAC system. Energy consumption for the high-energy case is not only much greater than for that of the low-energy building, it also shows a more dramatic difference between day and night. Furthermore, while consumption for the high-energy case is constant at around 30 kilowatts throughout the year, consumption for the low-energy case varies as a function of daylight availability. In the winter, the low-

FIGURE 60A

HVAC energy use in January. *Source: RMI.*

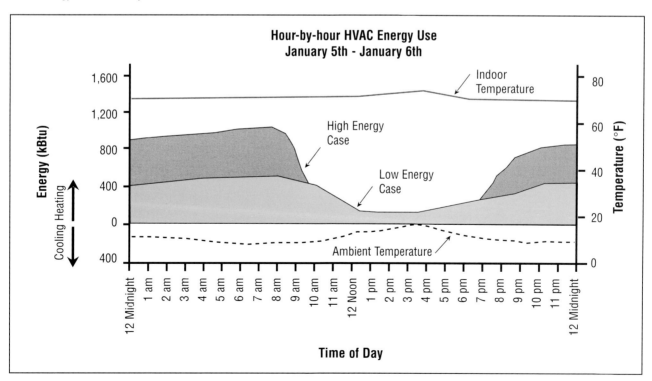

FIGURE 60B

HVAC energy use in July. *Source: RMI.*

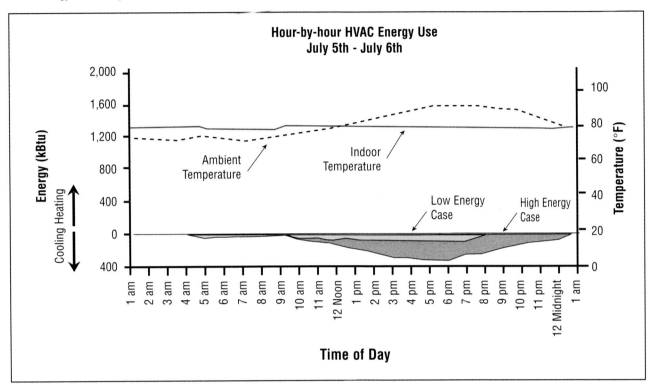

FIGURE 61A

Lighting energy use in January. *Source: RMI.*

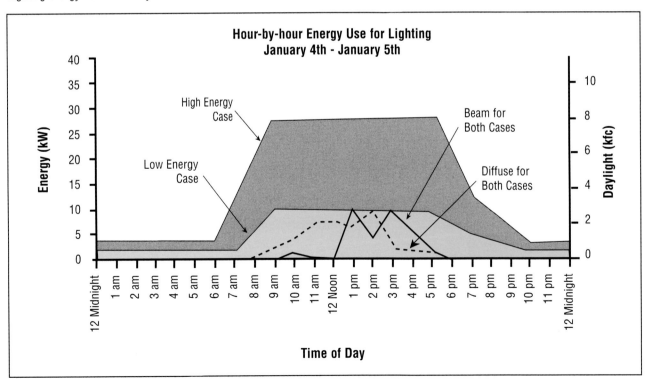

energy case requires about 10 kilowatts of electric lighting; in the summer, only about 7 kilowatts are needed. For the low-energy case, decisions regarding building orientation, window placement, and daylighting strategies all contribute to a more responsive and integrated building, resulting in lower energy use.

After individual components have been analyzed and optimized, it is helpful to look at their other effects, such as on electricity demand and emissions. For the MoDNR building, the success of integrated design on reducing electricity demand is substantial. All of the benefits of the site, water, material, air distribution, and daylighting features described earlier are contained in this and other big-picture graphs.

Figure 62 shows that the consumption graph for the low-energy case is relatively flat compared to that of the high-energy case. The high-energy case peaks markedly during the summer when demand charges are the most expensive. Note that the low-energy case in this graph does not include contributions from the solar photovoltaic panels on the roof of the MoDNR building. This PV system contributes about 2.5 percent of total building energy.

The emissions output (figure 63) for the MoDNR building illustrates reductions of more than 50 percent for all of the major pollutant categories. This observation is helpful in assessing a building's effects on both local air quality and climate change.

The MoDNR building is an excellent example of integrated design. Overall, it is 56 percent more efficient than the base case. While numerous cost-effective design strategies contributed to the success of the project, team collaboration also played a

FIGURE 61B

Lighting energy use in July. *Source: RMI.*

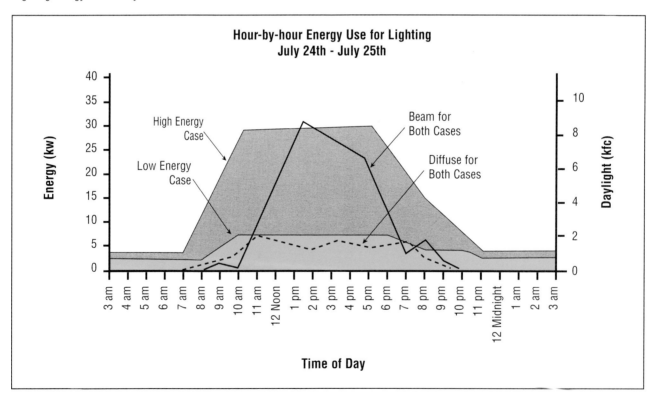

FIGURE 62

Monthly electricity demand. *Source: RMI.*

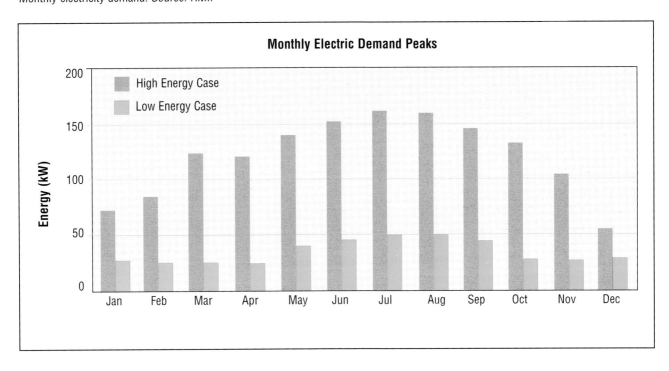

FIGURE 63

Annual emissions. *Source: RMI.*

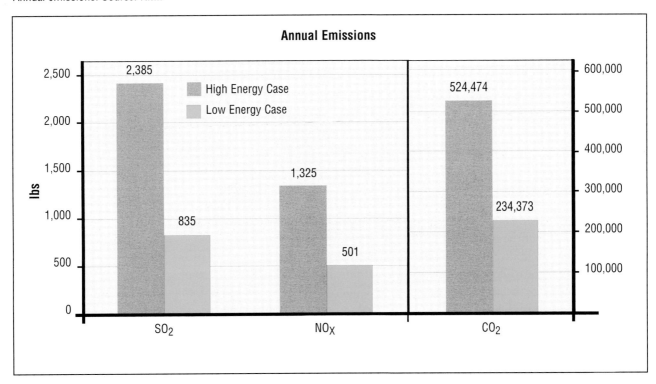

major role. A kick-off charrette that defined project goals got the project on the right track. Later, an inspired construction team exceeded expectations.

Economic Analysis

Because this is a government building, budget was a major concern. Tasked with creating the "greenest" building the budget allowed, the design team explored every potential avenue for savings. As a result of the large energy savings, the $17-million-dollar project will save the state $85,000 to $92,000 per year in energy expense. Estimated energy cost for this building is $0.81 per square foot [$8.72/m²], which compares favorably to $1.50 per square foot [$16.15/m²] for other state office buildings.

LEED Certification

The MoDNR building received a LEED Platinum certification. Figure 64 details the points achieved in each of the six LEED categories.

BARRIERS TO CREATING A HIGH-PERFORMANCE BUILDING

Integrated design is often misunderstood. The term does not refer to the careful coordination of structural components with ductwork and electrical wiring. Nor is it a project delivery mechanism intended to reduce construction time. Rather, it is a process dedicated to whole-system thinking aimed at optimizing building performance. Educating integrated-design participants about these common misperceptions may help them to better understand and champion the process.

Integrated design will not succeed if no one takes leadership responsibility for its implementation. This may seem obvious, but, too often, no one takes on this important role. As a result, "Some parts of the system are optimized or sized at the expense of others and of the overall result, but the tradeoffs are seldom made explicit. Instead, each successive designer's product is tossed over the wall to the next designer, as if the effort were not a team play but a relay race." (Lovins 1992) Designating a champion or facilitator is absolutely essential to generating a whole-building design.

Moreover, the building manager must be included in the project team. A common barrier to creating a high-performance building is inadequate attention to building commissioning and operation. This occurs because most team members are usually sufficiently satisfied with a building once it is built; they rarely revisit constructed projects to investigate how performance might be improved. Voluntary follow-up is probably not in most architects' job descriptions. However, building monitoring and performance enhancements *are* important to building managers, so they should be part of the project team from day one.

And, finally, integrated design cannot succeed if adequate time for it is not properly allocated. Integrated design requires additional time during the earliest phase of the project, sometimes before design even begins. Understanding and planning for this high-level effort is critical and must be included in project schedules. Many firms are finding that front-loading the design effort in this way offers benefits to the project beyond meeting the goals of environmental sustainability. The early collaboration produces a shared understanding of the project and its goals that can produce better-coordinated design and documentation in the later phases. Also including a

FIGURE 64

LEED scorecard for Lewis and Clark State Office Building. *Source: RMI.*

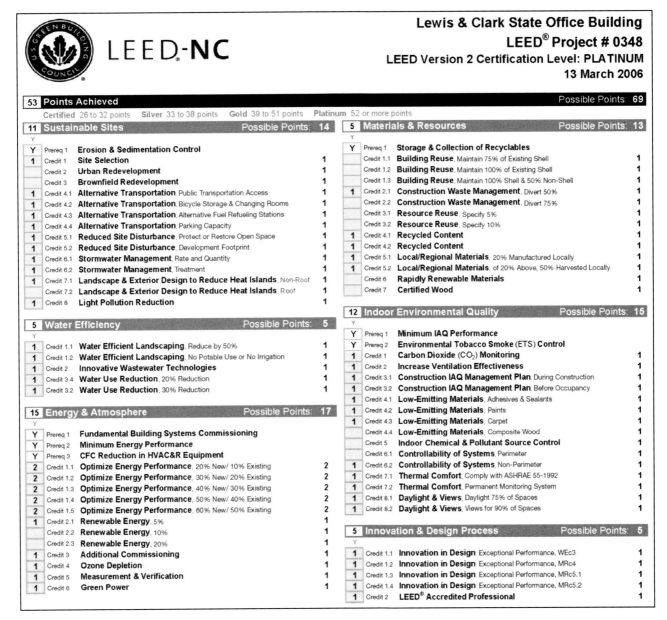

commissioning agent in the process has been shown to reduce the problems that arise in the initial period of occupancy. All of these factors affect the overall scope of work and must be adequately compensated in project fees and budgets. While this can increase the overall design fees, the resulting building performance will more than pay for this cost. In many cases, there are financial incentives and/or grants that can be used to help defray these added design costs.

Integrated-design can result in high-performance, low-impact, low-cost buildings. Applicable to all buildings types in all climates, integrated design is a fundamental concept available to all designers. Moreover, integrated design is essential to designing and constructing carbon-neutral buildings. Technology and new materials provide limited efficiency gains; without an integrated approach to building design, achieving carbon neutrality will be difficult. Integrated design is a highly cooperative, synergistic, and potentially enjoyable process that can result in elegant, economical, and environmentally sound buildings.

ABBREVIATIONS

AIA	American Institute of Architects
ANSI	American National Standards Institute
AP	Accredited Professional (LEED)
ASHRAE	American Society of Heating Refrigeration and Air Conditioning Engineers
BEES	Building for Environmental and Economic Sustainability
BREEAM	British Research Establishment Environmental Assessment Method
Btu	British thermal unit
CASBEE	Comprehensive Assessment System for Building Environmental Efficiency
CIR	Credit interpretation ruling
CIWMB	California Integrated Waste Management Board
CNU	Congress for New Urbanism
CO_2	Carbon dioxide
CRI	Carpet and Rug Institute
DOE	Department of Energy
EERE	Office of Energy Efficiency and Renewable Energy
EIA	Energy Information Administration
EPA	Environmental Protection Agency
FAR	Floor area ratio
Fc	Footcandle
FSC	Forest Stewardship Council
GBI	Green Building Initiative
GHG	Greenhouse gas(es)
GSA	General Services Administration
GWP	Global warming potential
HBA	Homebuilders associations
HUD	U.S. Department of Housing and Urban Development
HVAC	Heating, ventilating, and air-conditioning
IAQ	Indoor air quality
IEQ	Indoor environmental quality
IESNA	Illumination Engineering Society of North America
IRR	Internal rate of return
kWh	Kilowatt-hour
LCA	Life cycle analysis
LCI	Life-Cycle Inventory

ABBREVIATIONS

LEED	Leadership in Energy and Environmental Design
LEED-CI	LEED for Commercial Interiors
LEED-CS	LEED for Core and Shell
LEED-EB	LEED for Existing Buildings
LEED-H	LEED for Homes
LEED-NC	LEED for New Construction
LEED-ND	LEED for Neighborhood Development
LPD	Lighting power density
MMTC	Million metric tons of carbon
MoDNR	Missouri Department of Natural Resources
MTC	Metric tons of carbon
$MTCO_2E$	Carbon dioxide equivalents
NAHB	National Association of Home Builders
NELHA	Natural Energy Laboratory of Hawaii Authority
NIBS	National Institute of Building Sciences
NIST	National Institutes of Standards and Technology
NPV	Net present value
NRDC	Natural Resources Defense Council
NREL	National Renewable Energy Lab
O&M	Operations & Maintenance
PCB	Polychlorinated Biphenyl
ppm	Parts per million
PTAC	Packaged terminal air conditioners
PV	Photovoltaic
RFP	Request for proposals
ROI	Return on investment
SFI	Sustainability Forestry Initiative
SHGC	Solar Heat Gain Coefficient
SMACNA	Sheet Metal and Air Conditioning Contractors' National Association
SRI	Solar reflectance index
SWA	Steven Winter & Associates
USGBC	U.S. Green Building Council
VCT	Vinyl composition tile
VOC	Volatile organic compound

Abbaszadeh, S., L. Zagreus, D. Lehrer and C. Huizenga. "Occupant Satisfaction with Indoor Environmental Quality in Green Buildings." *Proceedings of Healthy Buildings 2006, Lisbon.* Berkeley, California: Center for the Built Environment, University of California. 2006.

American Institute of Architects (AIA). *High Performance Building Position Statements.* Washington, DC: AIA. 2005.

Deru, M. and P. Torcellini. *Performance Metrics Research Project–Final Report.* Technical Report NREL/TP-550-38700, National Renewable Energy Laboratory. 2005. (http://www.nrel.gov/docs/fy06osti/38700.pdf).

Edminster, Ann and Sami Yassa. "Efficient Wood Use in Residential Construction." New York: Natural Resources Defense Council. 1998.

Fowler, K.M., A.E. Solana, and K. Spees. *Building Cost and Performance Metrics: Data Collection Protocol, Revision 1.1,* Pacific Northwest National Laboratory. 2005. (http://www.wbdg.org/pdfs/fowlerbldg_costperf_metrics.pdf).

Gleick, Peter H., et al. "Waste Not, Want Not: The Potential for Urban Water Conservation in California." Pacific Institute for Studies in Development, Environment, and Security. November 2003.

Hawken, Paul, Amory Lovins, and L. Hunter Lovins. *Natural Capitalism: Creating the Next Industrial Revolution.* New York: Back Bay Books. 2000.

Heaney, James P. et.al. "Nature of Residential Water Use and Effectiveness of Conservation Programs." *Colorado Water.* October 1998. (http://bcn.boulder.co.us/basin/local/heaney.html).

Heerwagen, Judith. "Do Green Buildings Enhance the Well Being of Workers?" *Environmental Design and Construction.* January 30, 2001.

Hutson, Susan S., et al. *Estimated Use of Water in the United States in 2000.* U.S. Geological Survey Circular 1268. 2005.

Kats, Gregory. "The Costs and Financial Benefits of Green Buildings." A Report to California's Sustainable Building Task Force. October 2003.

Loftness, Vivian, Volker Hartkopf, Beran Gurtekin, Ying Hua, Ming Qu, Megan Snyder, Yun Gu, and Xiaodi Yang. *Building Investment Decision Support (BIDS™) Cost-Benefit Tool to Promote High Performance Components, Flexible Infrastructures and Systems Integration for Sustainable Commercial Buildings and Productive Organizations.* Carnegie Mellon University Center for Building Performance and Diagnostics. 2005.

BIBLIOGRAPHY

Lovins, Amory. "Energy-Efficient Buildings: Institutional Barriers and Opportunities." E-SOURCE. 1992.

Malin, Nadav and Alex Wilson. *Environmental Building News*. "Forest Certification Growing Fast." April 2003.

McGraw Hill Construction Research and Analytics. "Green Building SmartMarket Report." Lexington, MA: McGraw-Hill. 2006.

New Buildings Institute. *Advanced Buildings Energy Benchmark for High Performance Buildings.* 2005. (http://www.newbuildings.org/).

Pogrebin, Robin. "7 World Trade Center and Hearst Building: New York's Test Cases for Environmentally Aware Office Towers." *New York Times.* April 16, 2006.

Riley, D.R. and M.J. Horman. "Delivering Green Buildings: High Performance Processes for High Performance Results." *Proceedings of the Engineering Sustainability 2005 Conference.* Pittsburgh, PA. 2005.

Rocky Mountain Institute. "Tunneling Through the Cost Barrier–Why Big Savings Often Cost Less than Small Ones." Rocky Mountain Institute Newsletter, Volume XIII, Number 2, Summer 1997.

Romm, Joseph. *Lean and Clean Management: How to Boost Profits and Productivity by Reducing Pollution.* New York: Kodansha America, Inc. 1994.

Sanguinetti, P.E., Jennifer. From a PowerPoint presentation by Keen Engineering. 2003.

Society for Environmental Toxicology and Chemistry (SETAC). Guidelines for Life-Cycle Assessment: A Code of Practice. Brussels. 1993.

Stein, Richard G. *Handbook of Energy Use for Building Construction*, U.S. Department of Energy CE1220220-1. March 1981.

Steven Winter Associates. "General Services Administration LEED Cost Study, Final Report." October 2004. (http://www.wbdg.org/newsevents/news_040105.php).

Torcellini, P., S. Pless, M. Deru, B. Griffith, N. Long, and R. Judkoff. *Lessons Learned from Case Studies of Six High-Performance Buildings.* National Renewable Energy Laboratory Technical Report NREL/TP-550-37542. June 2006.

Turner, Cathy. *LEED Building Performance in the Cascadia Region: A Post Occupancy Evaluation Report.* Cascadia Region Green Building Council. (http://www.cascadiagbc.org/). January 2006.

U.S. Climate Change Technology Program. "Technology Options for the Near and Long Term." (http://www.climatetechnology.gov/library/2003/tech-options/index.htm). August 2005.

U.S. Department of Energy (DOE). *2005 Buildings Energy Data Book.* 2005. (http://buildingsdatabook.eren.doe.gov/default.asp).

U.S. Department of Housing and Urban Development. "Formaldehyde Emission Controls for Certain Wood Products." U.S. CFR Title 24—, Section 3280.308. 1985.

U.S. Green Building Council. "Eco-Friendly Builders Starting to Grow." USGBC press release. February 20, 2006. (http://www.usgbc.org/News/USGBCNewsDetails.aspx?ID=2158&CMSPageID=159).

U.S. Green Building Council. *LEED Reference Guide.* (http://www.usgbc.org/).

U.S. Environmental Protection Agency. *Cleaner Water Through Conservation.* EPA 841-B-95-002. 1995. (http://yosemite.epa.gov/water/owrccatalog.nsf/852887bbc1ca359585256ad400705867/9966f279e237efd885256b060072328c!opendocument).

U.S. Environmental Protection Agency. *ENERGY STAR* Overview of 2005 Achievements. March 2006.

Vitruvius. *Ten Books on Architecture.*

Wolff, Gary. "Beyond Payback: A Comparison of Financial Methods for Investments in Green Buildings." *Journal of Green Building.* Vol. 1, No. 1, Winter 2006.

Zung, T. *Buckminster Fuller: Anthology for a New Millennium.* New York: St. Martin's Press. 2001.

N C A R B

PROFESSIONAL
DEVELOPMENT
PROGRAM

SUSTAINABLE
DESIGN II
QUIZ

SUSTAINABLE DESIGN II QUIZ

INSTRUCTIONS

An answer sheet and a return envelope are enclosed with this monograph for your use in completing the following quiz.

When answering the questions, you may refer to the monograph or other reference materials as necessary; however, you must answer the questions without the assistance of others. NCARB will not give advice or clarification on questions.

Upon completion of the quiz, fold the answer sheet where indicated, and return it to NCARB in the supplied envelope, making sure to affix proper postage.

Within 10 working days from receipt at the Council office, you will receive a pass/fail score report. Failing score reports will be accompanied by a new answer sheet and envelope so that you may retake the quiz. NCARB recommends that you undertake additional study of the monograph before retaking the quiz.

This quiz is available online and we encourage you to take advantage of this time-saving option. If you pass—results are immediately processed—you can print your certificate of completion without delay. The enclosed flier provides additional details about NCARB's online monograph quizzes.

Please retain the score report for your records and for submission to those state boards requiring continuing professional development for license maintenance. Duplicate copies of the report are available to you upon written request.

Quiz scores will be maintained for five years by NCARB and will be made available only to participants and registration boards.

QUESTION 1

The LEED-EB rating system can be valuable to architects in an ongoing understanding of:

    A. operational practices during design.
    B. new building maintenance systems.
    C. the environmental impact of materials.
    D. the energy benefits due to LEED certification.

QUESTION 2

What is the key distinction of LEED-H certification versus the other LEED rating systems?

    A. It does not require an accredited professional.
    B. It is much easier to score the ratings under this certification.
    C. It recognizes only multifamily and affordable housing.
    D. It is managed regionally rather than by the national USGBC office.

QUESTION 3

Which two of the following credit categories were added to the LEED-H rating system?

    A. Energy and Atmosphere
    B. Location and Linkages and Homeowner Awareness
    C. Materials & Resources and Sustainable Sites
    D. Environmental & Controls and Builder Commissioning

QUESTION 4

In the LEED-H rating system, a controversial credit available within the Materials and Resource category is for:

    A. the design of repetitive developments.
    B. houses that are located on a brownfield site.
    C. houses that are smaller than the national average.
    D. the use of commercial green building products.

QUESTION 5

The innovative development of the LEED-ND rating system reinforces the importance of which of the following?

    1. Proximity to public transit systems
    2. Development of remote infrastructure
    3. New road construction to reduce commute times
    4. Localized shopping with large sprawling communities

        A. 1 only
        B. 1 and 3 only
        C. 2 and 3 only
        D. 1, 2, 3, and 4

SUSTAINABLE DESIGN II QUIZ

The three major versions of the LEED Accreditation Exam include separate emphases on:

    A. New Construction, Home Construction, and Neighborhood Development.
    B. New Construction, Commercial Interiors, and Existing Buildings.
    C. New Construction, Commercial Construction, and Existing Buildings.
    D. New Construction, Interior Construction, and Neighborhood Development.

The "textbook" for the Accreditation Exam is the:

    A. USGBC Reference Guide.
    B. LEED Reference Guide.
    C. LEED Accreditation Candidate Handbook.
    D. USGBC Accreditation Candidate Handbook.

The acronym "LEED" stands for:

    A. leadership in engineering and energy development.
    B. leadership in energy and environmental design.
    C. leadership in enhancement of environment design.
    D. leadership in engineering of ecological development.

In reaction to the perceived high cost and effort needed to LEED certification, a simpler self-assessment tool was introduced by the Green Building Initiative and is known as:

    A. Built Green.
    B. Green Globes.
    C. Earth Craft House.
    D. Energy Green Building.

When a project demonstrates leadership in energy and environmental design practices and a commitment to continuous improvement and industry leadership, the Green Globes assessment credits that project with what percentage of its rating scale?

    A. 35 percent - 54 percent
    B. 55 percent - 69 percent
    C. 70 percent - 84 percent
    D 85 percent - 100 percent

Some critics argue that LEED should give more credit than it currently does for which product?

    A. Wood
    B. Linoleum
    C. Cotton
    D. Steel

QUESTION 12

Florida's Green Commercial Building Designation addresses unique state conditions and adds credits for:

A. disaster mitigation.
B. renewable resources.
C. graywater irrigation.
D. tourism energy conservation.

QUESTION 13

Integrated design is a front-loaded design process that approaches the building as an interactive system that sets measurable performance goals:

A. without sophisticated mechanical controls.
B. with creative problem-solving techniques.
C. with interdisciplinary collaboration.
D. without environmental impacts.

QUESTION 14

Integrated design criteria consists of:

A. past building system failures.
B. suppliers and manufacturers.
C. architects, engineers, and environmentalists.
D. form, function, time, economics, and the environment.

QUESTION 15

Integrated design decisions that have the greatest influence on life-cycling performance occur:

A. when architects are the facilitators.
B. when building commissioning takes place.
C. during discussions at the beginning of the project.
D. as energy savings are measured during the first year.

QUESTION 16

Integrated design is composed mostly of strategies rather than defined phases because it is:

A. linear and fragmented.
B. linear and continuous.
C. nonlinear and fragmented.
D. nonlinear and continuous.

QUESTION 17

The first step in the integrated design process is to understand and define the:

A. user's needs.
B. critical issues.
C. design team members.
D. base case energy costs.

SUSTAINABLE DESIGN II QUIZ

QUESTION 18

To reduce costs and improve whole-building performance, it is imperative to identify:

    A. synergies among systems.
    B. qualified commissioning agents.
    C. the newest in sustainable materials.
    D. optimum uses for individual components.

QUESTION 19

What is critical to the design of an integrated building that quantifies benefits of design synergies?

    A. The owner's operating costs
    B. User feedback
    C. Future energy costs
    D. The energy analysis

QUESTION 20

In the Denver office building example, which of the following design elements is the largest contributor to reducing energy costs?

    A. Insulation
    B. Daylighting
    C. HVAC controls
    D. Efficient light fixtures

QUESTION 21

Which of the following are energy simulation tools?

    1. Energy Plus
    2. Energy-10
    3. DOE-2
    4. NREL

    A. 1 and 2 only
    B. 1 and 3 only
    C. 2, 3, and 4 only
    D. 1, 2, 3, and 4

QUESTION 22

Which two of the following are key differences between conventional building design and integrated building design processes?

    1. Use of design charrettes
    2. Distinctly different design phases
    3. Perceived duration of the project
    4. Required level of team commitment

    A. 1 and 2 only
    B. 1 and 4 only
    C. 2 and 3 only
    D. 3 and 4 only

QUESTION 23

Which of the following financial calculations used to compare investments in green building is defined as the ratio of the added cost of a feature divided by the expected annual savings benefit?

    A. Net present value
    B. Internal rate of return
    C. Simple payback
    D. Life-cycle return

QUESTION 24

Which of the following financial calculations used to compare investments in green buildings expresses life-cycle costs based on a set time horizon?

    A. Simple payback
    B. Net present value
    C. Internal rate of return
    D. Ammortized payback

QUESTION 25

Which of the following financial calculations used to compare investments in green buildings is expressed in terms of "income" generated by the life-cycle saving from the additional investment?

    A. Simple payback
    B. Net present value
    C. Internal rate of return
    D. Ammortized payback

QUESTION 26

Little or no added cost to high-performing green building designs on large building projects is achieved by using:

    A. triple glazing.
    B. extra insulation.
    C. integrated design.
    D. sustainable phasing.

QUESTION 27

According to the Capital E study commissioned by the California Sustainable Building Task Force, the average cost increase for all 33 LEED-registered and certified projects under study was:

    A. $2/sq ft.
    B. $4/sq ft.
    C. $6/sq ft.
    D. $8/sq ft.

QUESTION 28

The energy savings in green building design primarily come from a reduction in:

    A. heat gain.
    B. electricity purchases.
    C. fossil fuel consumption.
    D. heat loss.

SUSTAINABLE DESIGN II QUIZ

In California, as in most regions, the highest demand for electric power typically occurs during:

A. summer afternoons.
B. summer evenings.
C. winter afternoons.
D. winter evenings.

QUESTION 30

The Capital E study commissioned by the California Sustainable Building Task Force concluded that the requirements of green building design increased:

A. productivity.
B. working hours.
C. hourly rates.
D. utility rates.

QUESTION 31

The GSA study for the new courthouse concludes that even the lowest level of LEED certification results in a savings of:

A. $2.10/sq ft.
B. $1.20/sq ft.
C. $0.76/sq ft.
D. $0.26/sq ft.

QUESTION 32

The California Capital E study commissioned by the California Sustainable Building Task force investigated:

A. insulation values.
B. building costs.
C. HVAC systems.
D. energy costs.

QUESTION 33

Which of the following focused on first cost only and compared projects that were seeking LEED certification with those that were not seeking certification?

A. Sustainable Cost Comparison
B. Rate of Return Study
C. Davis Langdon Cost Study
D. Simple Payback Analysis

QUESTION 34

Which of the following professional groups was the first to advocate for environmental sustainable design?

A. AIA
B. NCARB
C. USGBC
D. ASLA

QUESTION 35

AIA's Committee on the Environment awards recognition to green building designs that successfully:

A. list surveys of architects, engineers, and construction firms.
B. promote integration of sustainability in curricula for education.
C. document measurable contributions to the health of humankind.
D. combine technical, environmental, and aesthetics performance.

QUESTION 36

Which of the following was the first state to offer tax credits to developers who build green buildings?

A. Oregon
B. Washington
C. New York
D. Pennsylvania

QUESTION 37

Which of the following states has adopted green design standards for government funded construction?

A. Oklahoma
B. Kansas
C. Minnesota
D. Nevada

QUESTION 38

Requirements for LEED certification have been applied in the municipal-funded building projects of:

A. Philadelphia, PA.
B. Austin, TX.
C. Reno, NV.
D. Memphis, TN.

QUESTION 39

The USGBC reports that over 25 percent of the clients of LEED-registered projects are:

A. state government agencies.
B. state public schools.
C. federal government agencies.
D. for-profit corporations.

QUESTION 40

The AIA is promoting a 50 percent reduction in the consumption of fossil fuels to construct and operate buildings by the year:

A. 2010.
B. 2015.
C. 2020.
D. 2025.

SUSTAINABLE DESIGN II QUIZ

QUESTION 41

Which of the following local governments provides incentives for LEED accredited buildings through expedited permit review?

A. Chicago, IL
B. Washington, DC
C. Boston, MA
D. Los Angeles, CA

QUESTION 42

Based on Figure 5B, the current number of LEED accredited professional architects is:

A. 1,000.
B. 2,000.
C. 3,000.
D. 8,000.

QUESTION 43

Based on Figure 5B, the current number of LEED accredited professional mechanical engineers is:

A. 1,900.
B. 2,900.
C. 3,900.
D. 5,900.

QUESTION 44

Based on Figure 4, the number of LEED accredited projects in the year 2006 is:

A. 1 200.
B. 1,700.
C. 2,400.
D. 4,700.

QUESTION 45

The major regional market in the United States for LEED-certified buildings is the:

A. Southeast.
B. Northeast.
C. Northwest.
D. Southwest.

QUESTION 46

Which of the following is an off-the-shelf technology that results in improved energy savings in many parts of the country for both housing and commercial construction, but is seldom used?

A. Low-E glazing
B. Performance roofing
C. Weather stripping
D. Lighting controls

QUESTION 47

The U.S. Green Building Council was founded in the year:

A. 1990.
B. 1993.
C. 2000.
D. 2005.

QUESTION 48

Based on Figure 2, the projected green building high end market value in the year 2010 is:

A. $10 billion.
B. $15 billion.
C. $20 billion.
D. $25 billion.

QUESTION 49

A fundamental reason for the development of the LEED Green Building rating system was to:

A. translate the goals of sustainability into design criteria.
B. develop a design awards program for green buildings.
C. determine if new construction has a negative impact on the environment.
D. provide building owners with guidelines to comply with federal regulations.

QUESTION 50

Which of the following is the primary difference between the LEED Green Building rating system and the British Research Establishment Environmental Assessment Method (BREEAM)?

A. BREEAM uses metric standards to evaluate buildings while LEED uses imperial standards.
B. BREEAM was designed to jump-start sustainable design in the United Kingdom.
C. LEED focuses on buildings in design while BREEAM focuses on completely constructed buildings.
D. LEED is a government-required program while BREEAM is a program of voluntary participation.

QUESTION 51

The U.S. Green Building Council is accurately described as:

A. a federally funded program.
B. a volunteer-driven program.
C. a state and local regulatory authority.
D. an organization started by AIA and the ASEC.

SUSTAINABLE DESIGN II QUIZ

QUESTION 52

The LEED-NC rating system evaluates buildings and project types against how many categories?

    A. 4
    B. 6
    C. 8
    D. 10

QUESTION 53

One of the most common mistakes made when pursuing LEED certification is:

    A. waiting too long to "go green."
    B. overestimating the potential number of credits.
    C. underestimating the added cost to the project.
    D. using the wrong rating system to evaluate a project.

QUESTION 54

Which of the following is a significant lesson learned about green design by the architects who designed the Artists for Humanity EpiCenter in Boston, MA?

    A. It is difficult to accomplish in an urban setting.
    B. It required sophisticated building systems.
    C. It could not have been built without tax credits.
    D. It does not have to be expensive.

QUESTION 55

What is the primary difference between the LEED-NC and the LEED-CI rating systems?

    A. LEED-NC uses different categories than LEED-CI to evaluate a project.
    B. LEED-NC has a higher percentage of points available for indoor air quality.
    C. There is a different proportioning of points between the various categories of the two systems.
    D. LEED-CI is associated with greenfield sites

QUESTION 56

When pursuing LEED-CI certification, which of the following must be performed to ensure the correct products have been used to obtain LEED credits?

    A. Writing of specifications
    B. Conducting preconstruction conference
    C. Submittal review and approval
    D. Commissioning

QUESTION 57

In the LEED-CI rating system, which of the following categories is allotted the greatest proportion of potential points toward certification?

    A. Water Efficiency
    B. Sustainable Sites
    C. Energy and Atmosphere
    D. Indoor Environment Quality

QUESTION 58

A unique aspect of the LEED certification for Core and Shell is the:

    A. opportunity it provides for tenants to qualify for LEED-NC status for its fit-up.
    B. incentives it provides for owners to increase lease rates.
    C. ability it provides to developers to qualify the building for "precertification."
    D. way it enables builders to reduce their construction costs.

QUESTION 59

The LEED rating system for Existing Buildings is used to evaluate the performance of:

    A. an adaptive reuse project.
    B. an occupied building.
    C. a renovated building.
    D. a building addition.

QUESTION 60

The LEED-EB rating system in its current form requires a comprehensive assessment of the:

    A. core and shell.
    B. roof and walls.
    C. heating and lighting controls.
    D. operations and maintenance.

QUESTION 61

The LEED-EB rating system differs from LEED-NC because LEED-EB has:

    A. fewer categories and credits.
    B. additional categories and credits.
    C. fewer prerequisites and credits
    D. additional prerequisites and credits.

QUESTION 62

Which of the following is NOT a LEED rating system?

    A. LEED for Renovations
    B. LEED for New Construction
    C. LEED for Core and Shell
    D. LEED for Neighborhood Development

QUESTION 63

The acronym "BIDS" is defined as:

    A. a cost benefit tool to promote performance components for buildings.
    B. a contractor support organization to provide green pricing.
    C. the building industry design system.
    D. a process to determine a building's illumination, daylighting, and sustainability.

SUSTAINABLE DESIGN II QUIZ

QUESTION 64

Which of the following terms is defined as the difference between the average monthly temperature and 65° F [18.3° C] multiplied by the number of days in the month?

    A. Btu Day
    B. Degree-day
    C. Solar intensity
    D. Energy use intensity

QUESTION 65

The water use in a building is difficult to predict because:

    A. human behavior varies.
    B. water pressure affects water use.
    C. fixtures often vary in their water use.
    D. water rates vary widely in the United States.

QUESTION 66

According to the U.S. DOE 2005, buildings use what percentage of all the energy produced in the United States?

    A. 22 percent
    B. 28 percent
    C. 39 percent
    D. 43 percent

QUESTION 67

According to the U.S. DOE 2005, buildings use what percentage of all the electricity produced in the United States?

    A. 39 percent
    B. 58 percent
    C. 66 percent
    D. 71 percent

QUESTION 68

Which of the following terms is defined as normalized energy consumption, based on building size?

    A. Energy intensity
    B. Embodied energy
    C. Source energy
    D. Vitruvius ratio

QUESTION 69

An ENERGY STAR program rating of 75 indicates that the building:

    A. uses 75 percent of the maximum energy used by similar U.S. buildings.
    B. uses less energy than 75 percent of all similar U.S. buildings.
    C. uses more energy than 75 percent of all similar U.S. buildings.
    D. is 25 percent from being a "zero energy" building.

QUESTION 70

Through the year 2005, there have been how many ENERGY STAR qualified new homes built in the United States?

    A. 225,000
    B. 350,000
    C. 525,000
    D. 750,000

QUESTION 71

The ratio of total energy use between residential and commercial buildings is approximately:

    A. 25 percent : 75 percent.
    B. 35 percent : 65 percent.
    C. 50 percent : 50 percent.
    D. 75 percent : 25 percent.

QUESTION 72

According to Figure 11, which of the following lists the building types by their building energy intensity (kBtu/SF), from lowest to highest?

    A. Office, food sales, warehouse, mercantile
    B. Mercantile, office, food sales, warehouse
    C. Warehouse, mercantile, office, food sales
    D. Food sales, warehouse, mercantile, office

QUESTION 73

The largest energy use in office buildings is for:

    A. heating.
    B. cooling.
    C. lighting.
    D. telecommunications.

QUESTION 74

The measure of a lighting design's efficiency is its:

    A. lighting power density.
    B. embodied energy use.
    C. site energy intensity.
    D. source energy intensity.

QUESTION 75

In the United States, buildings account for approximately what percentage of total water consumption?

    A. 15 percent
    B. 20 percent
    C. 25 percent
    D. 30 percent

SUSTAINABLE DESIGN II QUIZ

QUESTION 76

The energy efficiency rating program, ENERGY STAR, was first developed to promote energy-efficient:

    A. computers.
    B. appliances.
    C. homes.
    D. offices.

QUESTION 77

According to the LEED Reference Guide, v2.2, the water deficit in the United States on an annual basis is estimated at:

    A. 3,300 billion gallons.
    B. 3,500 billion gallons.
    C. 3,700 billion gallons.
    D. 3,900 billion gallons.

QUESTION 78

In all cases, an overall goal for a sustainable design is to:

    A. replenish potable water with rainwater treatment.
    B. consistently minimize the use of potable water.
    C. treat graywater to create potable water.
    D. combine treated graywater and rainwater for potable use.

QUESTION 79

Which surface runoff coefficient is the most effective in absorbing storm water?

    A. 0.05
    B. 0.10
    C. 0.50
    D. 1.00

QUESTION 80

In the LEED Life Cycle Assessment process, the term "life cycle" refers specifically to a comparison of the:

    A. environmental impact of different materials.
    B. durability of different materials.
    C. time to replenish different materials.
    D. cost of different materials.

QUESTION 81

Which of the following acronyms represents a software developed by the National Institutes of Standards and Technology for selecting cost-effective, environmentally preferable building products?

    A. CEEP
    B. BEES
    C. SCEE
    D. PSEE

QUESTION 82

The term "proxy metrics" refers to:

A. individual characteristics that contribute to the overall environmental assessment.
B. materials that may be substituted to achieve the appropriate LEED scoring requirements.
C. the rounding of nominal measurement to achieve LEED global standardization.
D. calculations required at the time of a LEED project submission.

QUESTION 83

Credits for LEED salvaged materials fall under the resource category of:

A. Reused.
B. Recycled.
C. Restored.
D. Replenished.

QUESTION 84

The term "embodied energy" refers to:

A. energy that is used to extract, process, or manufacture a building material.
B. energy saved by insulating ductwork in a building HVAC system.
C. a comparison of fuel sources that influence the environmental effects of energy.
D. the harnessing of excess energy within a building's various energy systems.

QUESTION 85

The LEED rating system category of Materials and Resources rewards the use of materials that were manufactured within how many miles from the project site?

A. 300
B. 400
C. 500
D. 600

QUESTION 86

Bio-based wood that is grown on FSC-certified property warrants which of the following?

A. All wood is harvested in an environmentally responsible, socially beneficial, and economically viable way.
B. All wood is harvested in a local ecology region, is a renewable source, and is pesticide free.
C. All wood is harvested meets local codes and the National Institutes BEES standard.
D. All wood harvested meets or exceeds the national standard for allowable moisture content and stability.

SUSTAINABLE DESIGN II QUIZ

Which of the following materials has the highest embodied energy in MJ/KG?

A. Glass
B. Galvanized steel
C. Copper
D. Aluminum

Which of the following is NOT an indicator when evaluating indoor air quality?

A. Lighting quality
B. Thermal comfort
C. Ceiling height
D. Building views

Occupants may describe the air in a room as "stuffy" and may become drowsy when the CO_2 concentration rises above:

A. 1,000 ppm.
B. 1,500 ppm.
C. 2,000 ppm.
D. 2,500 ppm.

Volatile organic compound (VOC) emissions in some products are regulated by:

A. local jurisdictions.
B. regional manufacturing associations.
C. state EPA offices.
D. federal agencies.